Praise

Back from Broken is. . . amazing! It is such a gut–wrenching account of one woman's courageous journey. I am thankful to have read it and am eager to share it with others. Huge kudos to JoAnn Marie for being willing to so honestly share her life experiences with all of us, and to give such glorious hope for better tomorrows!

Michelle Small
Colson Fellow

Back from Broken is both heart-wrenching and hope-inspiring. It exposes the tragic consequences of sexual abuse, but also provides practical, hope–filled guidance for long–term recovery to personal health and even flourishing. This book will prove valuable to the victims of sexual abuse and to others who wish to better understand and assist those who have experienced that trauma. JoAnn Marie's writing is clear, concise, engaging, honest, compassionate, and wise. She has handled an extremely difficult topic with an appropriate balance of candor and discretion. May God greatly use this book to bring immeasurable blessing to innumerable people.

Vance Christie
Pastor and author

As someone who has counseled hundreds of teens over the years, I have heard JoAnn's story countless times. What is unique is her sensitive and refreshing approach to healing the wounds of abuse. She lays out a path to releasing the bonds of slavery many fall victim to after the abuse is gone. I appreciate the sincerity of her message and her speaking the truth that ultimate victory comes from forgiveness and through taking responsibility for one's choices. I highly recommend this book not only for the victims of abuse to find a path to victory, but to anyone who wants to understand and support victims of abuse.

Chris Small
Colson Fellow

As a mental health practitioner, I hear the narratives of sexual abuse survivors. I also hear from survivors how they feel abandonment by God and question faith by saying "a loving God would never have let this (abuse) happen." This book helps survivors integrate a faith in God as well to see they *can* make a life worth living. A beautifully woven narrative of hope, faith, and choices.

Theresa Arnett Nickolaus

BACK
from
BROKEN

*A Journey of Healing
from Victim to Victor*

JOANN MARIE

MEDIA.COM

BACK FROM BROKEN

Copyright © 2022 by JoAnn Marie

Published by
Illumify Media Global
www.IllumifyMedia.com
"Let's bring your book to life!"

Library of Congress Control Number: 2022914741

Paperback ISBN: 978-1-955043-91-5

Cover design by Debbie Lewis
Author photo by fairy's fotography, November 2020

Printed in the United States of America

Dedication

For Ann Heiden, you knew it all and loved me dearly.

You never let me forget my loving God is in control.

Contents

Acknowledgments

My children, my greatest joy. You suffered under my brokenness but overcame to be godly parents and spouses. Thank you for forgiving me and loving me. I am very proud of you and love you deeply.

My children-in-law, thank you for loving my kids and standing by us all in our difficult times. May you find something in my story to encourage your own faith walk.

My grandchildren, I love you and am proud of you. I am always here for you, especially in my prayers. Remember our Awana years and continue to grow in faith and knowledge of God.

In memory of Jack (John) Hinze, ND, my dear mentor and physician, who kept me alive long enough to heal the pain and strong enough to endure all the hard times of life that have followed. I miss you.

Michael Sutton, ND, and Jeff Muilenburg, MD, for physical care and emotional support. I am blessed to have you as my medical team.

Dr. Russ Rapier, John Heiden, Dr. Bob Larson, Dr. Lisa Pattison, my psychologists and counselors, whose guidance directed and supported my healing journey for forty years through several major traumas.

Dr. Tanya Elgin, thank you for teaching me about Eye Movement Desensitization and Reprocessing (EMDR) therapy to help me lay some of my trauma to rest. I hope my recovery is an encouragement to others.

Pastor Vance Christie and Pastor Dan Starcevich, whose authorship is in a much higher class than my own. Yet you always took my calls, advised me graciously, and prayed knowingly. It is an honor to have your support.

My Bookers, Ann, Anne, Fairy, Jenn, Marlene, and Chris and Michelle. You prayed me through the process with godly wisdom and love and reminded me Satan does not want this story told though it is my important ministry to tell it. May we all rejoice to see people in heaven who trusted Jesus to heal them.

My friend Barb Hoff, who reentered my life for such a time as this to help me write for the broken ones, and for my book coach, Karen Bouchard, for teaching me professional writing.

Everyone at Illumify Media Global. I thank God Marlene Bagnull introduced us at the Rocky Mountain Writer's Conference. You are a tremendous company to work with on my first publishing effort. Your careful, professional guidance and Christian worldview brought my book ministry to life. Thank you.

My brother and sister, I love you and am proud of you. I am grateful for your friendship and loving support. You suffered as well. I needed to tell the truth, and I am sorry if it hurt you.

In memory of my parents. You taught me many important lessons. You made sure I learned about God, and He got me through the broken things. You set the example to consider all people valuable and to help others whenever you can. I'm grateful our later years were ones of reconciliation and admiration.

Timmy, I will see you in heaven.

For all others I didn't name, all my friends and relatives, past and present, who have walked through my life and left love and lessons behind. I gained important input on my journey to heal from each of you.

Foreword

Just to say the word incest is horrible. It is an evil word conjuring images of brutal adults hurting innocent children. And that is often how it happens. But when my friend, JoAnn Marie, asked for my advice on writing her story, I had no idea about the many other faces of child sexual abuse. The abuser can act kindly and lovingly, then turn on a dime and restrain and hurt. The abuse need not happen in a dark place hiding from view. It can happen driving down the road on family vacation. The child can be any age, but they experience the same confusion and shame. And it will follow them the rest of their lives.

JoAnn's story reveals many of the details of child sexual abuse including methods of grooming. Although her abuse happened fifty years ago, the relevance of this story is ripped from today's headlines. Comprehensive sex education, gender identity confusion, elective abortion, and human trafficking are all part of the pain and confusion revealed in her story.

However, her story does not stop in exposing the brokenness of sexual abuse. You sense no embarrassment as she tells of a lifetime of professional counseling she sought to cope with the aftermath of abuse. There is clear testimony of strength, healing, and guidance afforded her from her Christian faith. Yet, there is no pressure to follow her path. JoAnn Marie encourages you repeatedly to do the hard work to find your own path to healing and victory. There is hope in this story. I consider this book an important resource for my work in women's prison ministry and others who have suffered sexual abuse. I hope you will find the same sense of hope and healing my friend has experienced.

Barbara A. Hoff
High school English teacher

Introduction

You may be offended by the things I write. You may find me harsh, think I speak too much about private subjects, that I reveal too many repulsive details inside my story. I do not apologize.

I believe incest and sexual abuse deserve to be talked about openly. To do less simply adds to the shame, disgust, sorrow, rejection, and abandonment that accompanies sexual abuse. Sexual abuse is a difficult subject to discuss because it is a revolting, vile, disturbed, and reprehensible topic. Abuse becomes worse if kept in secret or spoken of in mild, benign terms.

Therefore, what you will read in the following chapters includes topics of torture and terror. I have included these details to give information about the people involved in my abuse to help you understand that from their own brokenness, they broke me.

You will read facts of the behaviors and conversations that happened between us as I remember them. These are my stories and memories. I have purposely avoided identifying people and places to protect others.

I want you to see examples in my life that may be the same as or similar to your experiences, whether from incest, child sexual abuse, rape, prostitution, or trafficking. I want you to know I care about what happened to you, or I would never have opened up my life to write this book. It cost me a great deal emotionally to recall these years. But I was willing to sacrifice my life for yours, if it will help you face your past and work toward healing. I most certainly did not always deal perfectly or righteously with the steps in my journey. That again should be an encouragement to you. No one is perfect, and no way is the perfect way to healing.

You will also read that my faith in Jesus Christ is the main reason I have survived and thrived for six decades after fifteen years of childhood sexual abuse. Because I believe Christian faith is the most complete answer to healing trauma and pain, I have included information at the end of each chapter to expose you to Christian resources. I chose Bible verses to reinforce the lessons I learned in my suffering. Because music can reach places words cannot, I have chosen two songs to offer you comfort and encouragement.

My hope is that you will read my story chapter and then the Bible verse. Sit for a few minutes and focus on any connection my experience has with yours. Use the Bible verse to take you to the full passage and read what else God says.

Perhaps as you discover how relevant the writings in the Bible are to our modern times, you will take advantage of the power and wisdom available through a personal relationship with the God of the universe. There is guidance inside on how to start that relationship. If not, you have lost nothing and have gained some knowledge and wisdom.

Listed after the Bible verse are song titles by artists I enjoy. There are many genres of Christian music. If you don't care for the ones I chose, look around for others. Look for the song titles online; I used YouTube music. Choose a music video that includes the lyrics so you can read the encouraging, loving messages from God and about God. These will strengthen you, settle your mind, and if you are like me, bring tears of gratitude for the miraculous ways the One True God can work to help you heal and forgive.

This book represents a lifetime of spiritual growth, decades of guidance and understanding from professional counselors, and, most importantly, the honest admissions of my hurts and my sins. It is hard work to heal but I am proof it is possible and well worth the time and effort.

I pray you will find the courage to begin your journey to health and healing. God bless you as you go.

JoAnn Marie

It is not our trust that keeps us, but the God in Whom we trust Who keeps us.

—Oswald Chambers

Prologue: A Sticker Stomachache

The dark doesn't bother me as much as the cobwebs.

As I lay tucked in with the canning jars on the cellar shelf, I feel the cobwebs stick to my hair. I know better than to reach up and pull at them because the daddy longlegs will get disturbed and come crawling.

I am well practiced at holding still when bad things are happening to me. In my six–year–old mind, I hope that if I do not respond to what is done to me, the person will stop what they are doing. I don't like the situation, but I cannot stop my body from physically responding to the fondling, and that makes me very angry. I do not like what is being done to me. In fact, I hate it, and my body reacts with a sticker stomachache.

The pain feels like that of my bare feet when I step on Texas sandburs. No one would believe that, but that's how it hurts.

The sticker stomachache brings me to this cool, dark place. I find more refuge in our cellar than I do in our home.

I come here to lie quiet and wait for the stomach pain to go away. I come here to escape what goes on above. I come here to pray, again.

"Dear God, please send someone to take me away. I know how to clean and cook. I can babysit. I'll do anything they want if they will just let me live with them. Please, God. I know you can stop it. Please stop it. Amen"

I try to keep the sticker stomachaches a secret. The day the pain happened at school my teacher made me stay in for recess until my mom came to take me to the doctor. I lay on the classroom floor holding my stomach and prayed again. I thought maybe the doctor would understand why the ache came and find someone to take me home to live with them.

But the doctor did not find anything wrong. "Take her home and feed her some prunes. It's probably constipation. She'll be fine in the morning."

No, I won't, I wanted to scream, not if he comes in the night again.

The sticker stomachaches follow the nights of pain and shame. My whole life is affected by the abuse. Why don't grownups recognize my trouble? Why don't I tell someone? Why isn't God answering my prayers of deliverance?

Read and Meditate

Be merciful to me, O God, be merciful to me, for in You my soul takes refuge; in the shadow of your wings I will take refuge, till the storms of destruction pass by. (Psalm 57:1–2 ESV)

Listen

"I've Never Been Out of His Care" by Joni Erickson Tada
  "He Will Hold Me Fast" by Keith & Kristyn Getty

Mother is the name for God in the lips and hearts of little children.

—WILLIAM MAKEPEACE THACKERAY

CHAPTER 1

They Named Her Nellie

Broken parents break children. For that reason, I will begin with the story of Nakleh (pronounced NUCK-lee), my mother.

Nakleh slipped inside their small hut, the thin wood door swinging on silent leather hinges. She made her way across the dirt floor, endeavoring not to awaken her mom and younger sister. She knew how far away her goat hair sleeping rug lay from the entrance. She moved quietly around the center support post, often a tool of torture, which held up the thatch roof. The roof was sealed against bugs with cow manure she collected from neighboring fields. The moist pieces of manure were used for mortar, the dried pieces for fuel for cooking fires.

Her small Lebanese village had a community oven, a clay igloo shape in the center of town, available for bread baking in order of social standing. Abandoned women went last when the coals had cooled, and the bread results would be inferior.

The village had no electricity, toilets, or running water. Each day Nakleh walked a mile to the river to draw a gallon–size clay jar of water and carry it home on her head. This abuse on her growing bones would lead to a spinal neck fracture later in life. She would spend her final years with body–wide neuropathy, resulting in loss of function of arms, legs, and bladder, a life akin to that of a quadriplegic.

The abuse was not only at the hands of her mother. At the beginning of her life in 1933, she had been subjected to a barbaric torture inflicted on infants to determine whether they were good or evil.

The naked infant, less than six months old, was presented to the village spiritual leader. He lay the child prone on a wooden board, exposing their tiny back to his sharp knife. He scored the child's back with deep gashes from shoulder to waist causing their blood to flow freely. It was thought that any evil spirits residing in the child would flow out with the blood.

Then the infant was laid face up in a barrel of ground salt to stanch the bleeding of the freshly inflicted wounds. If the infant survived this torture, they were deemed good enough to live. If they succumbed to the trauma, they were deemed evil, and it was better for the village they were dead.

My mom bore those scars on her back her entire life.

What scars were on her mind?

Three abandoned women, my grandmother, my mother, and her sister, lived in a culture where women had no worth without a husband. Nakleh's father had served in the French army in World War II as an ally to the United States. Allied soldiers were granted legal immigration to the United States and offered legal citizenship for their children, on the condition that the children arrive before their fifteenth birthday. At the end of his military service, he returned home long enough to impregnate his wife, then left for America, leaving his two–year–old daughter and unborn child behind.

My grandmother was a mean, envious, practicing witch who traded evil spells with another witch in the village. This behavior served to ostracize the family even more, as well as inviting more demonic activity into a tiny home already full of evil.

Being rejected by her husband left my grandmother angry, and she took that anger out on her two young daughters. Her discipline methods included tying them to the center support post of their hut for hours while she was away from home; placing hot peppers in their young vaginas; withholding what meager food was available; and sending them out on their own to receive insults and ridicule from the villagers.

Finally, she sold them into marriage. At age fourteen, my mom was sold to a thirty-two–year–old man who wanted to immigrate with her to America. He wanted to use her prom-ised citizenship to move to Texas and get rich raising cattle. The marriage took place in a neighboring town. A photo taken that day shows a group of stern and stiff adults, all men, some dressed as Syrian Orthodox priests, and my mom, front center, wearing a dark dress, head bowed and face hard.

Soon after the marriage service, Mom ran into the nearby forest and spent the night avoiding capture. She snuck back home ready to tell her mother she refused to go live with the man.

At some point, my mom had found a bundle of envelopes hidden in the ceiling rafters addressed to her and her sister. Throughout their lifetime, her father had written letters to them telling them of his love for them and his plans to bring the family to America.

Her mother had never showed them the letters.

Nakleh began making her own plans.

Her husband had purchased a ticket for her to travel by ship to New York. He would join her after she had secured her immigration papers. But instead of bringing her husband over, she planned to find her father. After all, in his letters, he said he wanted her with him. She would finally have a chance to escape her horrible life. She wrote him of her plans and asked him to meet her at the port.

In 1948, Nakleh boarded the ship with three men from a nearby town who were to be her sponsors for the six-week voyage. They fulfilled their duty by walking her up the ship's gangplank and checking her in, then left her, never to be seen again.

She was given a bed in the lowest deck in a room with many other women and children. She did not speak English, so when she was asked what food she wanted to eat, the only words she knew were "onion" and "chocolate." She arrived at Ellis Island, near New York City, sick and thin from starvation.

The immigration agent at Ellis Island could not understand her when she said her name was Nakleh. He wrote her first name as Nellie, taking away her real identity. Passing through the gate of the quarantine building, she expected to run into the arms of her long-awaited father. But it was not to be.

A tall Arab man approached her saying, "I am your uncle. Your father was shot in a poker game and is dead. I am here to take you to my home."

So began a three-year journey through several homes. In some she was no more than a slave, a few would give sanctuary, and in one she would be assaulted.

She lived for a short time with the sister of her husband. The woman helped her file the necessary papers with the Syrian Orthodox Church to annul her marriage.

One widower uncle kept her as a housekeeper and cook, requiring her to spend long evenings playing cards with him. One night he attempted to sexually assault her. She knew where he kept a handgun and shot him. She waited on the lawn while the police and ambulance crew responded to her phone call for help. The uncle's son arrived to take her to another family, defended her to the police, and apologized for what his dad had done. The uncle lived and did not bring charges against her.

She eventually made her home with a Lebanese-Italian couple who had three young children. She acted as their nanny and worked in their grocery store. They became her family, and she called the children her brother and sisters.

Before she left Lebanon, my mom had been prepared to attend Beirut University. She was a very good student, and this was a remarkable opportunity for someone from her background. However, when she registered for public school in the United States, she was placed in the fifth grade as a fifteen-year-old. Because of her size and maturity, most classmates thought she was a teacher.

While Nakleh did not speak English, she did speak French and with the help of a French-English dictionary, completed all the coursework for grades five, six, and seven in one school year. She eventually learned English and completed eighth grade as a seventeen-year-old. She entered high school also at age seventeen. Because of her grocery store job, she usually studied from 10 p.m. to midnight or later. She did not participate in after–school activities. She was able to complete one grade a year and graduated from high school in 1954 at age twenty-one, the same year she married my dad.

Throughout her life, she valued education. She enrolled in a community college after her three grown children left home, taking night classes in English writing, basic computer skills, business accounting, and business management. Although she attended classes periodically for many years, she did not accumulate enough credits to earn a degree. She was seventy-five years old when she enrolled in her last computer class.

Her grandson installed a personal computer and printer in her home so she could practice her computer drills outside the classroom. He gave her lessons on how to use the internet to research for her writing classes and explained how to use email to communicate with family. She had a hard time remembering all the necessary steps. She would often inadvertently poke a button or change a setting that ruined his well laid out instructions. She was very curious and envious of people who effortlessly used computers and cell phones. She had little success with technology herself.

Before her death, I established a scholarship in her name at the same community college at which she had studied. The scholarship is restricted to women with children pursuing a degree in business. Every semester, she would be so excited to see the reports with the names of the women who had received money to help make a better future for themselves and their children.

A strong will, hard work, and determination enabled Mom to survive life in a primitive Lebanese village. And it prepared her for a difficult life making ends meet on a meager income during many years of her marriage. She planted a large vegetable garden and canned the produce. She cleaned houses and a neighboring church. She took in ironing in an era when tablecloths and sheets were ironed along with men's shirts and ladies' dresses. She baked baklava and Syrian bread for sale. She sold handmade cream cheese mints for weddings and graduations. She worked as a school office secretary and then progressed to retail sales and management. For a decade, she and Dad managed motels in Missouri, Nebraska, and Wyoming. She retired at age seventy-eight but continued an active volunteer career for several years.

I, along with my siblings, were at her bedside when she died at age eighty-six. A truly remarkable woman went to her heavenly home. I am certain thousands mourned her death for she cared for and counseled people all her life.

She recognized their suffering because of the suffering she had known.

Yet, she was not able to recognize mine.

A father holds the keys to his daughter's feminine identity, her sense of self-worth, and her future relationships.

—Dr. James Dobson

CHAPTER 2

He Joined a Carnival

Born the tenth child of thirteen, my dad's birth in 1931 set him on the timeline of history to experience the Great Depression, World War II, and the Korean War. Dad said his hometown had once been named Grimville after his family. According to legal records, it's not true, but it felt like it could have been. My grandparents had thirteen children born between 1920 and 1936. Nine survived to adulthood, six men and three women. They produced fifty grandchildren.

Dad's family roots were in Prussia, and their surname was Grimm. The family immigrated to America in 1753, settling in Pennsylvania. There is a family legend that years later several families migrated west to Ohio. The men stood on a bluff and made a pact. Some would stay in the east and spell their name Grimm. The others would go farther west and use the name Grim. In this way, they hoped some of the clan would survive to preserve the name. The first recorded name change was in Indiana in 1855 by my great-grandfather.

Dad had three younger brothers. One day they were playing in the yard around the large water tank used by Grandpa's mules. Dad's two–year–old brother fell into the stock tank and drowned. As the oldest in the group, Dad felt the responsibility for his brother's death his whole life. He was five years old.

My grandpa had several work enterprises, and his sons were expected to help. He had two farm trucks used to haul cattle, crops, sand, and rock. The three older boys drove the truck until they left home to serve in World War II. While the older boys were away, Dad took over the trucking. His ten–year–old legs were too short to reach the clutch and accelerator, so Grandpa nailed boards to the pedals to make them taller.

Mules were used for farm work. My grandpa trained and sold them. Mules are dangerous to work with, but Dad was expected to help with feeding and watering the herd. In fact, my grandpa died at age seventy-eight of a head injury as the result of a fall from a mule he was training.

While the older children worked inside and outside the home to earn money for the family's provisions, Dad became Grandma's kitchen helper. My aunt told me Dad was very kind and considerate of his mother and they had a close relationship. His kitchen skills earned him a job in the army in the mess hall. He bragged he was the fastest potato peeler on the base.

When Dad was thirteen years old, he left home to join a carnival. Historically, a carnival life in 1944 would have been full of debauchery and illegal activities. Assuming a gypsy lifestyle at such an impressionable age surely exposed my dad to behaviors unbecoming for a young boy. Dad did not tell me specific tales of his carney days. I can imagine they would have been inappropriate to hear. I doubt very much he attended church, earned an honest wage, or lived a celibate lifestyle.

From the age of sixteen until he was drafted into the Korean War in 1952, my dad traveled with a troupe of adult men and women that sold magazines. Dad told me countless stories about this stage of his life. He worked in every state in the lower forty-eight and could tell me the characteristics of the main street in every state capital city. But from these stories, I doubt his lifestyle was much different from his carney days.

Based on my talks with Dad, I got the impression he did not live a sexually pure lifestyle during those years. Perhaps he was even the victim of unwanted sexual encounters from the older people around him. I gave him the benefit of the doubt.

Nevertheless, the troupe arrived in Charleston, West Virginia, in 1951. They stopped into the grocery store where my mom worked, and her beauty caught my dad's attention. He bought many bottles of Pepsi, returning daily to convince my mom to go on a date with him. She refused for several weeks. Finally, he told her he had his orders to report to army basic training. She agreed to ride the bus with him to see him off.

The nineteen months Dad spent in South Korea were difficult. The harsh winter caused frost bite to his feet that troubled him the rest of his life. The ammunition explosions caused a significant hearing loss.

He was trained as an army medic, and his mind was fractured by the horrors of the injuries he saw. He felt proud to be a member of the ambulance crew involved in Operation Little Switch in 1953. Sick and wounded American prisoners of war were released at the Bridge of No Return near Seoul and transported to base for treatment. Many men died inside the ambulance, causing him even greater distress.

Dad arranged for his military paychecks to be mailed to my mom, against regulations, reserved for wives and mothers. He told authorities she was his fiancée. She received checks for two years and handed the envelopes to Dad when he returned to Charleston, unopened. She did not feel right about cashing any of the checks since they were in no formal relationship. Dad used the money to pay for wedding and honeymoon expenses.

They wrote letters to each other every week. The relationship between them grew more personal. When Dad returned to Charleston in 1954, they were married in a Syrian Orthodox ceremony performed in Arabic. Dad joked for years he took Mom's word that they were truly married since he didn't understand the priest.

My parents lived in Charleston for the first five years of my life. Dad had a variety of jobs including insurance and car sales, Orkin pest control, and security jobs. By 1960, there were three children, little work, and Dad was homesick for Nebraska. His mom told him men were being hired to build Calamus Dam near Atkinson, Nebraska. We left West Virginia and moved in with my grandparents.

It's a common occurrence for two women living in the same house to experience conflict. Putting two cultures together added to the stress. Dad was gone for weeks at a time working on the dam construction and not around to run interference. Eventually, my mom convinced Dad to move us. Unfortunately, it was to a decrepit, rundown farmhouse, and we were miserable.

Soon, Dad reacted to the stress with a nervous breakdown. Today we call it post-traumatic stress disorder. One night, he lay with his head on my mom's lap, talking incoherently, screaming that the men needed help. Mom watched his brown hair turn white overnight.

The next morning, she called the sheriff for help. When a deputy arrived, Dad shot him. Both men were transported to the hospital. The deputy recovered from his wound. Dad was admitted to the veterans hospital psychiatric ward in another city. He did not return home for six weeks.

Our family moved six times in the next ten years. Dad had trouble keeping a job and paying rent. When I was eight years old, the landlord came to collect. Dad ran outside to hide in the cornfield, telling us kids to hide under a bed in the living room and Mom to hide in the bathroom. It was scary to hear the landlord pound on the door demanding his due.

After he left, Dad borrowed a farm truck from someone and told us to pack up. My five–year–old brother and I carried boxes to the back of the truck for Dad to load. He built a fire in a barrel. If he deemed the box contents not worthy to take up the limited space in the truck, he threw the box in the fire. We children had very few toys, most of them gifts from our wealthy aunt. We watched in horror as Dad threw that box of toys into the fire, and the sparks flew into the night sky.

Later, my brother and I lay on top of the load as we drove down the highway to our next house. Back in Charleston, Dad had earned an award from his insurance sales. It was a black Samsonite folding table with four matching chairs. This was a prized possession, and the reward story was repeated each time it was brought out for guests to use. That night the table blew off the truck. It felt good to watch it go. For years Dad pondered over what happened to that table.

Dad's nickname was Doc, first because of his army medic experience, then as a first–aid technician in an ammunition factory, and eventually, as an orderly in two hospitals. His dream was to become a medical doctor, impossible without an education. However, after earning a graduation equivalent diploma in 1970, he became the first emergency medical technician (EMT) on a newly formed city ambulance crew. And with the new job came the first long–term home situation for our family. My parents were there twenty-five years.

It was common for the people of Dad's generation to react to their experience of the scarcity of the Great Depression by holding on to the smallest possession. Once my dad took the EMT job in 1970, he became a hoarder of foodstuffs and paper products. He had several six–foot shelves built in the basement of our home. He kept them filled with more canned food, soaps, and paper products than our family of five could use in a year. Forty years later when I moved them from their home to an assisted living apartment, I took two heaping carloads of groceries to charity groups.

His hearing loss and night blindness cut Dad's dream job off after eight years. Until retirement he worked security and car sales, headed a newspaper distributorship, and managed motels.

Watching out for others was a lifestyle habit for Dad. He served as deacon in every church he attended, which kept him aware of the felt needs of people in the congregation. Often, funds needed came from his pocket, even when the pockets were mostly empty. He and Mom had a weekly ministry to serve communion to shut-ins. He volunteered at the local hospital as a patient guide on admission as well as wheelchair assistant to appointments at the laboratory and x-ray. He was an avowed brother in arms to veterans and earned an award for 1,000 hours volunteering at the local veterans hospital.

Dad rarely passed by a car stopped along the roadside without stopping to assist. He was known to bring stranded motorists home to stay while auto repairs were made, often for several nights. He called upon his medical background performing first aid at accident scenes until authorities arrived. His kind, caring behavior always brought high praise from others. However, that was not the man I lived with.

Dad was known for flying an American flag in his yard. He had paid a great price for his military service. I believe raising his flag every morning was a reminder his sacrifice was worth it. His pride in our country and the military prompted me to create a family gift to a new military memorial park erected in one of the small towns our family had lived in. The funds were used to buy a flagpole for the center of the park and a name plaque set alongside. He died at age eighty-seven with full military honors at his funeral.

It was difficult to show respect for my dad with my history of abuse at his hands. However, my forgiveness of him, and God's grace, gave me strength and courage to do it.

I am the way, the truth, and the life.

No one comes to the Father except through me.

—Jesus Christ

CHAPTER 3

A Long Walk to Church

Church attendance was a regular occurrence in our family. We were there Wednesday nights and twice on Sunday with few exceptions. My dad was a church leader, Mom taught Sunday school, and my younger siblings and I sang trios during the service.

Our church building was a white wooden structure with the sanctuary on the main floor. Sunday school classes and potluck meals were held in the basement. My Sunday school classmates and I would fill in the blanks of our workbooks as we listened to the Bible lessons. I am thankful for the years I studied the entire Bible, cover to cover. Nothing was omitted for convenience or to avoid offending someone. I heard all the words God gave us in His Word, the Bible.

I enjoyed learning about the Bible. I learned to sit quietly for forty-five minutes and could find a verse in the Bible quickly. I memorized many Bible verses as a child, and they brought me comfort and instruction. Unfortunately, the circumstances of how I came to a personal relationship with Jesus are a bit jaded.

I was seven years old when my dad walked in as our substitute teacher. The lesson was one I had heard multiple times on the crucifixion and resurrection of Jesus. However, this day the Holy Spirit moved in my heart, and I realized Jesus had made that sacrifice for me. I knew I was a sinner and wanted to be forgiven and go to heaven when I died.

Dear reader, you can know that for sure, too.

Since the beginning of the world, the sin of Adam and Eve to disobey God's rules in the garden of Eden has passed down to every person ever born. Because God loves us and wants to have a personal relationship with each of us, He made a way to pay for that sin. He required the blood sacrifice of His only Son, Jesus, to be the payment. Jesus willingly gave His life on a cross and died. Three days later He rose from the dead, escaped His tomb, and spent fifty days with His disciples. He completed His teaching with them and returned to heaven. Then, the Holy Spirit came to live in each person's life who would believe that Jesus' death and resurrection was the payment for their sin. No longer separated from God by sin, we will be welcome in heaven where we will live with Him through all eternity.

In John 3:16–17 (TLB), Jesus explains it this way: "For God loved the world so much that he gave his only Son so that anyone who believes in him shall not perish but have eternal life. God did not send his Son into the world to condemn it, but to save it."

After the other kids left the room, I said to my dad, "I want to do that. I want to believe that Jesus died for me to pay for my sins." Dad helped me pray, and I placed my trust and faith in Jesus Christ.

My being led to Christ by my abuser did not minimize my experience. In fact, it reveals the great power of God to overcome evil. The truth of the Bible was greater than the chronic sin of my dad's abuse. Countless people have asked me through the years, "How can you even believe in God with all the terrible things you have been through?"

My answer is like Peter in John 6:68–69 (NLT): "Simon Peter replied, 'Lord, to whom would we go? You have the words that give eternal life. We believe, and we know you are the Holy One of God.'"

Believing in Jesus as my savior and friend at an early age has been an advantage in coping with life. Through the power of the Holy Spirit in my life, I have found strength and guidance to persevere through challenging times. I memorized Isaiah 26:3 (NLT) for support. "You will keep in perfect peace all who trust in you, all whose thoughts are fixed on you!" Yet, Dad's actions were hypocritical examples of a Christian's behavior.

My mom was a beautiful Arab who took great care with her dress and appearance. She was also very conscientious with her housekeeping. Invariably, she would try to get too much done before she dressed to leave the house. Chronically late to church was something Dad could not tolerate.

One Sunday morning, he flew into a rage and shoved her into a window, breaking it. Fortunately, Mom was not cut. I pulled on him to get off her and he threw me on the floor. He screamed at me to clean up the glass, while he dragged her into the bedroom to dress. His rage continued to escalate.

When we finally got to our car it would not start, so we began the four–block walk to church. I asked him to stop screaming because people in houses along the way could hear him.

"Stop making trouble!" he screamed as he pulled me down the street, kicking me repeatedly on my backside.

I was wearing a white dress with yellow polka-dots which became covered with black shoeprints. Of course, there was no going home to change. I was not wearing a sweater or jacket I could wrap around my waist to cover the dirt. I arrived at church feeling miserable and in pain. I walked backward into the sanctuary making excuses for my odd behavior until I could sit down.

My humiliation increased at the end of the service when I walked to the front of the church with the other congregants to receive communion from our church leaders, including Dad. The black shoeprints on my dress reflected the blackness in my heart. Because of this feeling of anger against my dad, I would have declined communion that day if I did not fear his reprisal. Our family appearances were foremost.

People like my dad had no business serving as a church leader and I knew it. We were hiding the sin in our home from our church friends. I like to believe someone would have helped us if we had only spoken of the abuse. Our silence perpetuated the sin.

It is important that we do not look to people to show us what God is like. Human behavior is often hypocritical. We talk one way and walk another. But the One True God, our creator, is all-loving, all-powerful, and all-knowing. We may not understand His ways, but we can trust Him. He cannot lie and He does not change.

My relationship with my dad could have tainted my view of my heavenly Father. By the grace of God, that has not been the case, for I believe the following truth: "And we know that all that happens to us is working for our good if we love God and are fitting into his plans. . . If God is on our side, who can ever be against us?" (Romans 8:28 and 31b TLB).

Listen
"Good, Good Father" by Casting Crowns
    "What a Friend We Have in Jesus" by Alan Jackson

Essentially loneliness is the knowledge that one's fellow human beings are incapable of understanding one's condition and therefore are incapable of bringing the help most needed.

—HUBERT VAN ZELLER

Chapter 4

Feelings of Worthlessness

I was a typical first–born child: driven, responsible, perfection-istic, bossy. I was also very loyal and protective of my younger siblings. I experienced physical and emotional illness from the screaming, rage, and beatings in our home. I assumed it affected the younger kids too, and I did what I could to protect them. Whether I begged our mom to quit screaming or pulled my dad off someone getting hit, I tried to shelter them.

Once, my brother and I rode our bikes a mile on a two–lane highway to the nearby river bridge. Mom was scared to death when she realized where her nine– and twelve–year–old kids were and came rushing to get us with the car. She loaded our bikes in the trunk and drove us home. Once there, she flew into a rage and began striking us with a belt.

I thought she was overreacting and out of control. I lay on top of my brother to take the beating so he could be spared the physical abuse, if not the verbal abuse. When I became a mother, I understood her concern for our safety. However, I still feel she overreacted because our ride took place on a clear, sunny day on a rural highway with very little traffic. It was only a mile from home.

My brother and I learned a strong work ethic in our Midwest village of 400 people. We helped Dad cut down and trim trees, haul trash from people's homes to the village dump, and cleaned a neighboring church. My brother and I split the town's newspaper route, and we each had fifty customers. We were both slight of build so balancing fifty papers on each of our bikes was precarious and difficult until we delivered some of the load.

I did many household chores including cleaning, ironing, and baking. I had Mom's German chocolate cake recipe memorized by age nine. I was often bitter about my house responsibilities because my brother and sister did not help very often.

My sister was five years younger and was not expected to do many chores. We shared a double bed, and I was mad at her for not waking up at night when Dad was abusing me. In my protective way, I did not want to interrupt her sleep, yet I wanted her to wake up and scare Dad off. She also made a habit of eating my favorite chocolate cake leftovers while I was at school. I felt very sorry for myself and was jealous of her for being the baby of the family.

My brother got out of chores because he spent much of his time with Dad. I was jealous of that too. It was easy for Dad to prefer to spend time with his son. And of course, even though I yearned for my dad's attention, it was always inappropriate and unhealthy when I got it, so our relationship was confusing to me.

The grading system in my era for school was A through F, A being the highest value of 100 percent. My parents expected us to get A's, and maybe one B. Despite my emotional distraction from abuse, I earned high grades at school. There were times after a night of abuse that I had a hard time concentrating and would get a low grade on an assignment, but it wasn't enough to pull down my average.

One example is a spelling test I took in the fourth grade. I was a star speller, and it was an easy subject for me. We memorized ten words a week and tested each Friday. One day the teacher called out the word *than* and I blanked. I simply could not visualize the word to write it down. I got teary and upset and did not concentrate on the next seven words she recited. I handed in a mostly blank paper. I was devastated. I did not have the maturity to understand the abuse was interfering with my concentration. I just thought I was stupid. It added to my feelings of worthlessness.

I developed other physical reactions to the abuse. Until age ten, I sucked my thumb when feeling anxious and was often teased by my peers. My parents tried to break the habit with nasty tasting lotions or spankings.

I've talked about my sticker stomachaches, the psychosomatic illness I developed from the abuse. Unfortunately, I also developed a lung disorder called pleurisy, which is an inflammation of the lining around the lungs resulting in sharp chest pain and shortness of breath. A common cause of the inflammation is a viral infection. At the time, the treatment was rest and a hot compress to the chest.

When I was a toddler, I was poisoned by breathing in the chemicals released during an explosion at a chemical factory in my neighborhood. I imagine that may have damaged my lungs and made me more susceptible to lung disorders. Whatever the cause, I suffered several attacks of pleurisy while in elementary school. I don't know if it was brought on by the stress of the abuse, but it occurred on a regular basis after an episode of molestation.

My first attack happened at school in the fourth grade. I collapsed on the floor next to my desk, struggling to breathe. I was taken to the family doctor for diagnosis and treatment, then sent home. I was to rest and apply a hot compress to my bare chest, which drew the attention of my dad. I was lying under the covers on my bed feeling scared, sick, and short of breath. Dad sat down very close to me, in effect, binding me to the bed with the covers. I felt trapped and claustrophobic. He wanted to use Vicks VapoRub on my chest and back to open my airways. I refused and fought him off. I was in no mood for more sexual molestation. Even as an adult I panic when I am covered with a heavy blanket and cannot throw it off quickly. I pray to calm myself until I feel safe.

My mom played a role in my feeling bad about myself too. She was a screamer. So much so, there were times I would beg her to hit me rather than scream at me. It gave me terrible stomachaches to hear her scream. I was very ashamed that as an adult I subjected my children to the same rage-filled screaming for many years.

I was jealous of the time my mom spent with other kids in town. Everyone loved her and wanted to be her friend. She had a gift for getting people to talk about their problems. Teenagers often visited our home to talk to her in private. While I cleaned a bathroom or washed dishes, she listened to my friends vent about their problems. I felt such ambivalence about the situation. I was proud when other kids would say, "Your mom is so beautiful and nice. You are lucky to have her." On the other hand, I resented the time she spent with them and not me.

I had to come to grips with the jealousy, bitterness, and hatred I felt toward my peers. They were getting the attention I wanted from my parents. My anger and bitterness were going to make me miserable and would have no effect on changing the situation. I asked God to help me, and it was a difficult battle. I quoted Psalm 23:1 (TLB), "Because the Lord is my Shepherd, I have everything I need!" I wanted to depend on God to be my parent and accept His unconditional love for me, not listen to Satan tempt me to anger.

Because of Dad's medical training, he rarely passed by a stranded motorist or accident scene without stopping to help. We kids knew better than to complain. The stop often took a long period of time. If we were on our way to an event, we were probably going to be late or miss it altogether. It seemed to me that stopping for other people was more important than what I needed. It made me feel worth less than a stranger. It made me angry because the stranger would come away thinking my dad was the nicest, kindest guy in the world. Then the man I knew would return to the car and there was nothing nice about him.

In the fifth grade, our school introduced students to band music by teaching us how to play a tonette, a flute–like instrument we call a recorder today. The class was going to play our songs in the school spring music concert. Our teacher asked me to be band director. This was a great privilege for me, and I was getting positive attention. Because I had taken piano lessons, I knew how to read music and keep tempo. I was nervous, but I was sure I had the necessary skills to do a good job.

It was a ten–mile drive on a main highway from home to the concert. Dad stopped for a stranded motorist. I pleaded with him to take me to school and come back, or to go to a nearby farm and call someone else to help the motorist. He didn't listen.

I got to the concert very near the end. My teacher was angry that I had not told her I wasn't coming. There were no cell phones in 1966. Even if I could have found a way to call the school, the phone was locked in the main office, and no one would have answered it. I was heartbroken at the missed opportunity. I did not tell my teacher the truth of why I was late. My parents did not try to explain either. Once again, I felt a stranger was more important than me, and it made me feel sad and worthless.

My Dad had several extramarital affairs. One day, he came to my room looking sad.

"I want to give you something very important. This ring is for you, my special girl. I want you to wear it all the time to remember how much I love you."

The ring had two square rubies, his favorite gemstone, on a narrow silver band. It was a pretty ring, but I knew the truth. He had bought it for a girlfriend who had broken up with him and given it back. There was no way I would ever wear that ring. I bore the emotional scars of being his special girl. There was no way I was going to wear a physical reminder of his sick relationship with me. I hid it in a box and sold it at a garage sale when I was thirty years old.

The chronic abuse made me feel bad about myself. It was hard to make friends and let them get close. I did not want them to know about the abuse. But in the sixth grade I let myself have one special girlfriend.

One evening, we worked together on a school project until dark. Dad thought she should not walk the two blocks to her house alone and offered to walk with her. I immediately felt uneasy.

"I'll go too," I offered.

"No, you need to get to bed," said Dad.

I was in my room when I heard him return home and turn on the television. A few minutes later, the phone rang, and I answered.

"Your dad kissed me! On the mouth! What is wrong with him?" my friend sobbed.

"I'm so sorry. Please don't cry, it will be okay. I'll be sure it never happens again." She hung up.

I ran to the living room and screamed, "What have you done? Can't you leave anyone alone?"

My mom entered the room and asked what was going on.

"Shut up," said Dad, "it's no big deal. She's making it up."

I was terribly sick to my stomach and went to bed crying, wondering how I would ever get through school the next day. But my friend never said a word.

Because I spoke freely with the boys at junior high school about sexual things, they went through a stage of window-peeking on me. One night while bathing, I saw a face at the bathroom window and screamed in fright. Dad went rushing out of the house to confront the boy. In the dark the peeper forgot about the wire clothesline he had ducked under when first arriving. As he ran away, his tall, lanky frame hit the wire at full run at throat level and dropped him flat on his back gasping for air. Dad thought it was funny and left the kid to suffer. He returned to his TV program screaming at me for encouraging the boy to come look at me. I was mortified to be seen naked and was very scared the boy was badly hurt. He and I did not discuss it, but the story got around school. Thankfully, the focus was on the funny fall and not his view in the window.

In high school, my openness with the boys to discuss girls and sexual matters was not appreciated by their girlfriends. I was relating to boys in the best way I knew, and it was inappropriate. But I got attention and they seemed to be my friends.

One morning in gym class several girls decided to teach me a lesson. As I gathered my books to leave the locker room, they jumped me and held me down while someone poured shampoo over my head. There was no time to get back in the shower to rinse it out. I spent the afternoon hours looking unkempt with greasy looking hair. It was very embarrassing. I was hurt to be treated that way. I could understand their anger, but my humiliation was great.

Later that afternoon, my English teacher tried to get me to explain to her what had happened to me, but I would not say.

"JoAnn, you are one of my favorite students. You pay attention. You do the assignments. I like your poetry. I hope you will continue writing and don't keep your feelings inside."

It was the nicest thing anyone had said to me in years.

Read and Meditate

For the LORD your God is living among you. He is a mighty savior. He will take delight in you with gladness. With his love he will calm your fears. He will rejoice over you with joyful songs. (Zephaniah 3:17 NLT)

Listen

"Who You Say I Am" by Hillsong Worship

"Glorious Unfolding" by Steven Curtis Chapman

We cannot treat the human embryo as cheap and worthless without passing judgment on all human life, including our own.

—MONICA FURLONG

CHAPTER 5
A Loss of Life

The chronic sexual abuse I was experiencing led me to a pattern of promiscuity from age twelve. I had boyfriends on a regular basis and was usually involved in some level of sexual activity. The older the boy, the more invasive the sex.

Experts will tell you that relationships built on sexual attraction have little lasting power. But I thought every boy I slept with was planning to marry me and everything would be good. I would get away from home. I would have someone who loved me for me and not what they could get from me. I was a very messed up girl.

By the time I was sixteen, I was pretty much a nymphomaniac, or sex addict. The boys enjoyed it for a time but even they saw I was out of control. Their parents were appalled at my public displays of affection. Along with the physical clinging would come emotional clinging, and soon the boys were gone.

You might wonder if I visited the local Planned Parenthood clinic for contraceptives. I did not. As I confessed to be a

Christian, and my desire was to obey God's directions, I did not want to admit I was planning to have sexual relations. I believed my activity was a sin; I should not condone it by being on birth control. Crazy thinking, I know.

As a seventeen–year–old senior in high school in 1973, I could see the end in sight for leaving home. I had wanted to be a nurse since I was a little girl and was making plans to attend Mary Lanning School of Nursing in Hastings in August.

I was our school choir president, and our production of the musical *Oklahoma* was in full swing. I was having trouble getting up in the morning for classes because I was extra tired. Also, my usual stomachaches were much worse. I didn't tell my parents I wasn't feeling well until I vomited blood. Our family doctor admitted me to the hospital for tests.

After two days of finding nothing abnormal, he walked into my room and in a very disgusted voice said, "There is nothing wrong with you. You're pregnant."

And turning on his heel, he left the room and me to contend with my stunned parents.

The first words out of my dad's mouth were "How can you embarrass the family like this?"

As usual my mom said nothing, but she did cry.

The next twenty-four hours were a blur. A nurse called a family meeting in a conference room. My boyfriend came and asked me to marry him. I said no. I did not want to give up my dream of being a nurse. I did not think a marriage of two teenagers had much promise to succeed.

Most of all, my dad was pushing for abortion. He asked a nurse friend to "talk some sense into me." Her daughter had recently been to the East Coast for an abortion, the closest location to us for legalized abortion. I was "so fortunate" because *Roe v. Wade* had passed recently, and a neighboring state was offering abortions for medical reasons threatening the life of the mother. Dad jumped on that information, got my blood typed and cross-matched, a requirement of the abortion clinic, threw me in our Buick, and took off for a six–hour drive across state lines.

There are snapshots I remember of that day. The abortion clinic felt like a regular doctor office. Several girls, not adult women, sat in the waiting room. I was taken into another smaller room with a desk. A very nice lady helped me complete my paperwork. When we got to the line Medical Reason for Procedure, I blanked. I did not know of a reason. I looked at her imploringly, "What do I say?"

She asked me several questions about my medical history and none of my answers satisfied her until I said I had gastro-intestinal X-rays to find a stomach ulcer last week.

"That's it! The x-ray might deform the baby and you could die in labor."

Did she really just call it a baby? Was I really going to die?

I went along with it and signed the papers. My baby was going to die so I could get on with my life and my dad would not be embarrassed. Really, really bad decision.

As I lay on the procedure table, I felt woozy from a drug I was given and drifted in and out of sleep. There was a poster of a koala bear above me on the ceiling. I wondered what Australia had to do with anything. And didn't koala bears have a pouch they held their babies in?

I heard the doctor say, "Male, ten weeks old, intact."

Then I woke to the sounds of moaning. I figured it was me, but I felt another presence. Opening my eyes, I saw I was on a gurney in a low–lit room with several other girls. The moans came from another girl and soon she was screaming out of control. She was whisked away, and I never understood what it meant or what happened to her.

I was eventually released, got in the Buick, and lay on the back seat. My pain and bleeding were manageable, and all I did was sleep. About three hours later I woke up confused, looked out the window in the dark night just as a road sign flashed by with the name of a nearby town on it. It was a town I had never heard of, and a sign I would drive by for the next forty years and get physically ill at the memory.

My boyfriend was waiting when I got home but I didn't want to talk to him. The pain was bad, but the shame and grief were devastating. I eventually attempted to overdose on a prescription tranquilizer to stop the remorse but was discovered before I could escape my regret.

My mom seemed to understand that my loss was like her miscarriages. But Dad screamed, "Get over it. It's not a baby." I never believed it. I knew I was a murderer.

Read and Meditate

For you formed my inward parts; you knitted me together in my mother's womb. I praise you, for I am fearfully and wonderfully made. Wonderful are your works; my soul knows it very well. (Psalm 139:13–14 esv)

Listen

"Stand in Your Love" by Bethel Music and Josh Baldwin
"His Mercy is More" by Keith & Kristyn Getty

You can never learn that Christ is all you need until
Christ is all you have.

—CORRIE TEN BOOM

CHAPTER 6

The Second Betrayal

The final weeks of high school were full of stress from college entrance ACT and SAT tests, applying for scholarships, performing in our final choir concerts, completing several term papers, working weekends at my waitress job, and staying away from my house whenever I thought my dad would be home. Being around him made me feel sick, anxious, and very angry. People outside our home thought he was the nicest, kindest Christian man you could want to know. Their high praise only made me feel less worthy.

One afternoon, I skipped out of school early to meet friends at the local racetrack. I was not a gambler, but I had a car and got positive attention when I offered to drive others to the track. It was also my day to give my mom a ride home from work. I made a quick stop at home before going to get her.

I flew in the front door and down the hall to my bedroom before I realized the television was on in the living room. I turned back to see my dad coming off the couch headed my way. Rather than be cornered in the narrow hall, I ran toward the front door but didn't make it in time.

Jerking me around by the arm, he threw me up against the door and snarled, "Where the hell do you think you're going in such a hurry?"

I stood mute.

"Answer me! Who are you going to meet?"

I didn't answer.

"Answer me, you little whore!"

From somewhere deep inside me, a fierce, harsh voice said, "Yeah, well, if I'm a whore, you made me one."

Anticipating the blow, I turned my body and took the hit aimed for my head on my shoulder. My fury was so great, I did not feel the pain. The swing took him off balance and he took a step back. That was my opening. I flung open the door and fled to my car, locking the doors. I threw it in reverse and sped down the street. Looking in my rearview mirror, I saw him standing outside screaming at me and I wondered, *Where am I going to sleep tonight?*

My hands were trembling on the steering wheel, and my fury was great. I could not believe I had finally stood up to my dad and wondered what it would cost me. How in God's name could my mom stay with a man like this? Why did she not take us all away and make this craziness stop? Was she truly oblivious to the abuse I was enduring? I drove to the employees' entrance and waited for her to come out of the store.

As she entered the car, she saw my tears and recognized I was very upset.

"What happened? What's wrong?" she asked with concern.

"Dad called me a whore. I hate him, I hate him! Why do you stay? Why can't you help me?" I cried.

In a meek and quiet voice, she asked, "Do you mean when he plays with you?"

I was stunned into silence. My chest hurt. I could not breathe.

In her mild vernacular, she had used the words *play with* to mean the sexual abuse I had endured for nearly fifteen years.

She knew.

My last parent had abandoned me. What was I to do now?

Read and Meditate

Fear not, for I am with you; be not dismayed, for I am your God; I will strengthen you, I will help you, I will uphold you with my righteous right hand. (Isaiah 41:10 ᴇsᴠ)

Listen

"He Will Hold Me Fast" by Keith & Krysten Getty
    "10,000 Reasons (Bless the Lord)" by Matt Redman

It is not within our power to place the divine teachings directly in someone else's heart. All we can do is place them on the surface of the heart so that when the heart breaks they will drop in.

—HASIDIC SAYING

Chapter 7

Heartbreak

I did not view my upcoming high school graduation as a day of celebration but one of escape. My mom was planning my graduation reception to be held in our home. All our friends and relatives knew she would prepare delicious food including some of our Lebanese desserts like her famous baklava. We would serve her delicious homemade cream cheese peppermint–flavored candy mints. And of course, she would do the extra work to personalize them in the shape of diplomas and mortar boards in my purple and gold school colors. Mom made beautiful sheet cakes, complete with butter cream icing, and handmade roses made with stiff frosting, adding lovely vines and leaves to complete the picture.

I did not want anything to do with the party. For me, it was another opportunity for our family to keep up the appearance of a happy, healthy home. I was sick of the lies.

But I was a liar, too. I lied to my parents for weeks getting permission to spend the night at a girlfriend's house who was hosting an all–night party for several classmates. With this lie in place, I would make an appearance at my reception but leave early to spend the night at my boyfriend's apartment. I was giddy with excitement. After dating for over a year, I was looking forward to our first breakfast together. I was so sure this relationship would be my escape from home.

I left my reception at ten o'clock leaving behind a furious mother and offended guests, not the least of whom was my cousin. He had come from out of state to share in my special event.

I was feeling very grown-up and excited as my boyfriend and I walked the grocery aisles picking out our favorite breakfast foods. I was living in a dream thinking how this would be my life for many years to come. Although the bond of our relationship was scarred by the aborting of our baby, I was confident we would have more children and live a wonderful life together.

Scientists say because of the strong hormone chemicals in the minds and bodies of teenagers, romantic attachments are especially strong. There is actual science behind the adage "You never forget your first love." It is a reason so many relationships are rekindled at high school reunions. I certainly believed our relationship was forever. I was desperate for love and acceptance.

However, the following morning after breakfast and lovemaking, I heard this.

"I'm done with this."

"What this?"

"You. I'm not going to go with you anymore."

"What are you saying? You can't mean it! You just finished making love to me! What is wrong with you?"

"Wrong with me? It's you! You're crazy! All you think about is sex. All you do is bitch about your parents. I'm done with this. I don't want you."

And he walked outside to his classic muscle car and sped away.

I was devastated, so sad, feeling abandoned, and so very, very ashamed.

What he said was true. I was a hot mess and he deserved better. I spent the next year proving him right as my sexual addiction burned through a new city of men while I attended nursing school.

Later that fall, I came home from nursing school for a weekend visit. I was driving around late at night waiting for my parents to go to bed so I could go sleep at home. I was feeling very lonely and sad, and my mind went to my old boyfriend. I was still deeply in love with him and wondered if there was any chance he would take me back. I had not changed anything in my life, but maybe I could fool him into thinking I had. I drove to his house and knocked on the door. The porch light came on and I saw him look out around the curtain.

I smiled broadly and waited. He did not smile, just shook his head slowly. He looked disgusted.

"Please, open the door. I just want to talk."

"Sure, you show up at midnight to 'just talk'?"

"Yes, I promise."

He let me in but did not close the door.

"What do you want?" he asked angrily.

"I want to know if you would go out with me again. I miss you so much. I'll try harder to be nice and not push you. I don't want to live without you anymore."

He just stared at me.

"Please, say something."

"Stay here," he said, and he walked into the bedroom.

A teenage girl was standing in the doorway wearing one of his t-shirts. She didn't say anything, just stared at me. I recognized her. She was a couple years younger than me and worked at the same restaurant we did. It was obvious they were in a relationship.

He reached up to a closet shelf and took down a framed photograph of me. It was an 8 x 10 I had made for his birthday gift to remember me by while I was at nursing school. Seeing it stored on a shelf, with a new woman in his bed, and this angry encounter made it clear he was not interested in rekindling our affair.

Handing me the picture he said, "Get out and don't ever come back here again."

I left in tears of humiliation, sorrow, and heartbreak. Once again, I knew he was being brutally honest with me. I was so very, very sad and lonely. I drove around for another hour before going to my parents' house. I simply could not face the possibility of my dad coming after me following this horrible event.

I did not know where to go for help to change the trajectory of my life. I knew what God expected from me, and my shame was intense. I returned to school the following morning with no hope.

This hopelessness was the result of my sin, not because God had abandoned me. I had a habit of lying to cover up my absences from school when I was tired from a night of carousing. I hid the guilt and shame I felt behind a facade of quiet happiness. I could not form healthy friendships with women because I did not want them to know the real me. I felt superior to them because I knew more about men and their needs.

Every time I had an illicit sexual relationship, a piece of my soul was taken by the man. The risk of disease grew with each encounter, not to mention another pregnancy. I put myself in dangerous, secluded situations where I was treated with disrespect, even enduring physical harm at times. I made these choices; I was not coerced.

As a Christian, I was wrong to disobey God's commands to avoid sex outside of marriage. I was reaping the consequences of shame, disease, pain, guilt, poor school grades, and loss of healthy friendships.

As a young child, I memorized the verse "While we were still sinners, Christ died for us" (Romans 5:8 ESV). Because I accepted Christ as my savior, I could claim the promise in 1 John 1:9 that if I would confess my sins to Him, God would forgive me and cleanse me from all of them.

In his book, *Gentle and Lowly*, Dane Ortland[1] writes that God loves us "on terms of grace and grace alone in defiance of what we deserve." While we build our lives on self-pride, glory, and pleasure, we close our ears to God. "It was then, in the hollowed–out horror of that revolting existence," Christ died for us. It was "a divine strategy planned from eternity past *to rinse muddy sinners clean and hug them into his own heart despite their squirmy attempt to get free and scrub themselves clean on their own*" (emphasis added). Jesus loved us enough to die to pay for our sins. At the point of our salvation, we become a new person in the eyes of God, worthy and loved. When we

---

1   Dane Ortland, *Gentle and Lowly: The Heart of Christ for Sinners and Sufferers* (Wheaton, IL: Crossway/Good News Publishers, 2021), 191.

sin after salvation, we do not lose God's love, but it certainly diminishes our relationship with Him.

I was not attending church or spending any time reading my Bible. I was depending on my past salvation and not growing in my faith or being with other Christians. With my feelings of shame and loneliness, I could have chosen to accept God's love and forgiveness and stop my sinful life. There were people around me who would help me, and the Holy Spirit would help me change. But I did not ask for help from God or man. I felt unworthy of help. In my self-loathing, I believed the lies of Satan, not the truth of God's love.

Read and Meditate
And hope does not put us to shame, because God's love has been poured into our hearts through the Holy Spirit who has been given to us. (Romans 5:5 ESV)

So then, since we have a great High Priest who has entered heaven, Jesus the Son of God, let us hold firmly to what we believe. This High Priest of ours understands our weaknesses, for He faced all of the same testings we do, yet He did not sin. So let us come boldly to the throne of our gracious God. There we will receive His mercy, and we will find grace to help us when we need it most. (Hebrews 4:14–16 NLT)

Listen
"Goodness of God" by Jenn Johnson (radio version)
"All My Hope" by David Crowder and Ed Cash

Child of God, you cost Christ too much for him to forget you.

—C.H. Spurgeon

CHAPTER 8

Out of the Frying Pan, into the Fire

Once I understood my mom was aware of the sexual abuse I had endured all my life, something in me shattered. If neither of my parents were going to protect me, I would distance myself from them. If I could not trust others to take care of me, I would trust only myself.

Once again, I would not tell anyone what my situation was so they could help me. I knew adults and classmates who would have taken me in if I had confessed to them what was going on in my house. The shame and secrecy of sexual abuse was keeping me in a prison of isolation and loneliness. I assumed that if people knew the type of abuse I had been a part of they would have rejected me, even blamed me for letting it continue so long. After all, I was now old enough to completely understand the inappropriateness of the sexual activity my father kept trying to push on me. Yet, I would not speak about it. And the silence made me feel even more dirty and unworthy.

Moving to another city removed me from the nightmare at home. It also gave me a new hunting ground for sexual encounters with men. Regular carousing in bars and cruising the strip resulted in one–night stands with men whose names I didn't know. The debauchery, disease, depression, and disgust over my behavior built and built up inside me.

One night after another illicit sexual encounter, I was overcome with guilt of the sin of my behavior. I believed God wanted me to live a life that would please Him and bring me happiness and contentment. Yet, my sinful lifestyle was causing depression and sadness because I had no healthy, loving, respectful relationships in my life. As the old adage goes, I was looking for love in all the wrong places. Because I would not ask someone for help in making changes, there seemed to be no way out of my pain. Thank God, I did not numb my pain with drugs or alcohol. I was not entangled in those addictions.

As I drove my car down the highway toward home, I accelerated over seventy miles per hour and yanked the steering wheel toward the ditch. I intended to plow into one of the roadside power poles and end my life. I had to stop this pain. But God had another plan.

I raised my hands skyward and cried, "God, forgive me!" and waited for the impact.

Miraculously, the steering wheel jerked, and the car swerved back onto the highway.

I slammed on the brakes, bringing the car to a stop on the shoulder, and sat and shook violently.

I had messed up again. I could not even kill myself.

And yet. . . I truly believed it was the hand of God that jerked the car away from the power pole. If He was not ready for me to die, He must have a plan for my life. I needed a drastic change if I was going to pursue another lifestyle. And the change came quickly.

My nightlife was preventing me from being successful in my college and nursing classes. My depression was creating problems relating to my instructors and patients. My grades did not meet the minimum standards to continue my studies. After seventeen months, I was expelled from nursing school.

The director of my nursing school saw great promise in my nursing skills. At my dismissal, she encouraged me to get my personal life under control so I could return to my studies. She offered me a chance to reapply if I would retake my science courses in another college. If I earned high grades, she would entertain a readmission interview in a year. It broke my heart to pack my car and drive away from the dormitory. My childhood dream to be a registered nurse was ended. I had no one to blame but myself.

For the first time in many years, I had developed friendships with several women in my class and now I had lost them too. I looked up to them. I wanted to tell them why I was so broken, but I simply could not say the words.

I hope you can understand how messed up my thought processes were at this time. It was easier for me to talk about my sexual exploits, acting as an unpaid prostitute really, than it was to admit I had been the victim of chronic sexual abuse. The sexual addiction was my responsibility. The abuse was not. But the deep scars of sexual abuse prevented me from admitting what had happened to me.

Any of these women would have understood and supported me in my recovery. Several were Jesus-followers and would have helped me return to healthy living. I did not give them the chance to help me.

Read and Meditate

Don't you realize that your bodies are actually parts of Christ? Should a man take his body, which is part of Christ, and join it to a prostitute? Never! And don't you realize that if a man joins himself to a prostitute, he becomes one body with her? For the Scriptures say, "The two are united into one." But the person who is joined to the Lord is one spirit with him.

Run from sexual sin! No other sin so clearly affects the body as this one does. For sexual immorality is a sin against your own body. Don't you realize that your body is the temple of the Holy Spirit, who lives in you and was given to you by God? You do not belong to yourself, for God bought you with a high price. So you must honor God with your body. (1 Corinthians 6:15–20 NLT)

Listen

"Surrounded (Fight My Battles)" by Michael W. Smith
   "Rise Up (Lazarus)" by Cain

If you bring up my past, you should know that Jesus dropped the charges.

—ANONYMOUS

CHAPTER 9
An Opportunity for Change

I chose to return to my parents' home until I could enroll in another college. I slept with a chair propped against my bedroom door to keep Dad out. I continued my habit of avoiding my parents. My younger siblings lived at home, and I made myself available to them. I took a job selling shoes in a local shopping mall for two months. Then I moved to another city for a semester to retake my science courses. I received the highest grade, interviewed for readmission, and started my junior year of nursing school in the summer of 1975.

That year, I began dating a man whose family owned a large farming corporation. I seduced him and the sexual activity became a monogamous relationship, which effectively shut down my dangerous lifestyle of one–night stands.

We eventually married, but the sexual activity in which we had engaged while dating had interfered with us establishing a strong friendship and developing a meaningful relationship.

At the time our wedding was being planned, it became obvious I would not tolerate having my dad walk me down the aisle. I could not stomach that kind of pretending. Without explaining the true reason for my plan, I convinced my parents that they would both walk with me, one on each side. Therefore, once again, saving face for the family and robbing me of a moment of happiness on my wedding day.

My pattern of hiding my shame behind looking proper to the public cost me much. My concern for others' feelings overshadowed my own needs. You may think loyalty and compassion for others are admirable traits, and you would be right. I, however, used them in an unhealthy manner. I often felt unworthy of putting my needs or wants before those of other people, which resulted in a lot of pretending that my life was going well.

Being married gave me distance from my parents and emotional support I needed to investigate how to bring criminal charges against my father. The statute of limitations was coming to a close. I discussed the matter with my younger brother who asked me not to pursue it and I agreed. If I was not going to go public with my problem and get some justice, I was going to have to find some closure.

At this same time, I was expecting my first child (not including the one I aborted). I was terrified that I would sexually abuse the child. I did not admit my fears to anyone, not even my husband. One day as I sat at my sewing machine patching my husband's work jeans, he stopped in and found me sobbing.

"What are you crying about?" he asked in surprise.

"I'm afraid to have this baby!" I sobbed.

"Well, you are going to," he said sternly, and walked out.

And that was the end of the matter. He shook me out of my emotional state and brought me back to reality. My selfishness and fear of my father had cost the life of my first child. I would not let my fears affect the life of my second.

I made an appointment with a Christian psychologist and began the long journey to heal the trauma of the abuse, the guilt of the abortion and sexual addiction, and to prepare myself to stop the cycle of sexual abuse in our family. Again, God intervened to quell my fears when my baby girl was born in 1978.

My husband and I were living in a rural home set amid thousands of acres of crops. Shortly after we moved there, I began to experience health problems from sensitivity to farm chemicals. Within five years, I was suffering many symptoms of muscle weakness, seizures, and great fatigue. I pushed myself to participate in caring for my home and family. I was involved in many areas of service in my local church, but I felt very sick most of the time. I tried to compensate for my physical pain—and the pain of isolation in my marriage—by taking care of others. I had good intuition to see when others had problems, and I enjoyed trying to solve them.

One example is a family in my church that lost their home to fire. I organized a place for them to stay and a fundraiser for cash needed to replace belongings. On another occasion, a young missionary couple was moving to a foreign country. I stayed awake all night helping the young mom sort through their belongings to select what they would need for the next several years away from shopping in the United States. There were smaller projects and organizations to participate in, but the focus of my life was other people. It helped me feel needed and gave me worthwhile activities to spend my time on.

My husband and I were married forty years with very little emotional intimacy, shared interests, or activities. At one point I became convicted of my seduction and apologized for disrespecting him and starting our relationship in an unhealthy way. He did not seem to understand where I was coming from, but it mattered not. I felt I had cleared my conscience and asked for forgiveness. I believe I am only responsible for my own relationship with God, not how others relate to God. I try to keep short accounts of sin and repentance. Being imperfect, I pray often for a right relationship with God.

Read and Meditate
Therefore, if anyone is in Christ, he is a new creation. The old has passed away; behold, the new has come. (2 Corinthians 5:17 ESV)

Listen
"Amazing Grace" (with a twist) by The Sound
    "Holy Water" by We the Kingdom

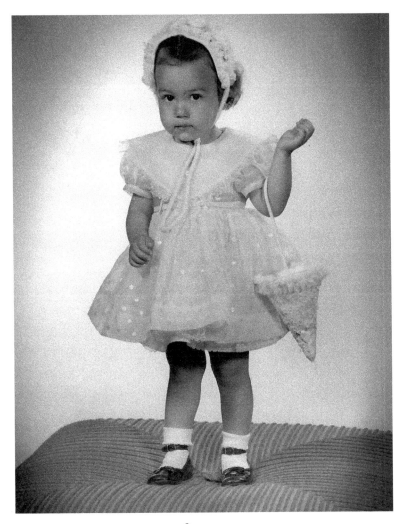

3 years

The expression on JoAnn's three-year-old face may reveal the sexual abuse that started as a toddler.

12 years
Pictured here in sixth grade,
JoAnn was the smallest girl
in class until puberty at age
fourteen.

19 years
Receiving her nursing
student cap in 1974 at
age nineteen was a dream
come true for JoAnn.

Nellie
Before immigrating to America, fourteen-year-old Nellie Abood was bound for higher education at the University of Beirut, Lebanon. However, US authorities set forth a set of circumstances that prevented her from completing high school until age twenty-one, pictured here.

JoAnn's Dad
His service during the Korean Conflict in the US Army from 1951-1953 was a point of great pride. He married Nellie a month after his discharge at age twenty-two.

*Time alone with God and faithful study of
His Word equip and establish us
so we can stand firm when Satan attacks our thoughts.*

—KAY ARTHUR

Chapter 10

Suicidal Thoughts

I have been at the brink of suicide three times.

I was wrong to contemplate it without turning to someone for help. Yet, it was God's will I not succeed from a tranquilizer overdose after my abortion. I know it was the hand of God that jerked the steering wheel of my car aside to prevent me from driving into a light pole after a night of heartbreak. I believe God woke my husband to interrupt me using his shotgun to try and stop the pain of facing another New Year's Eve with no hope for change.

I was a Christian who believed in God's power and promises. Still, I needed a human being who could help me apply all I knew to my circumstances and help me change myself. That person for me has been a Christian psychologist.

Making a commitment to professional counseling is an important decision. The expense alone requires a firm decision to make time for each session and to take time from other areas of life to process what is revealed. Once deep, or even hidden, psychological and emotional information is mined from your mind, you must do something with it. Talk is not enough. There must be an acknowledgment of the wrong done or pain experienced and how it makes you feel. You need to accept what role you played in the situation, even if you are the victim. It is important to speak all the truth.

You must decide you will change behaviors and thought processes that led you into the problem or kept you there. A counselor can help identify the lies you believe that keep you trapped in repeating the cycle of whatever heartache or addiction you deal with. It is important to make a promise to be accountable to another person who will help you meet your goals.

Healing is hard work. No one else can do it for you. Only God, through the Holy Spirit, can empower you with the strength and perseverance needed to succeed. You cannot substitute God's help and guidance with other earthly endeavors: drink, drugs, sex, work, exercise, mind games, video games, pornography. These things will fill up your time but not the emptiness in your heart and mind.

Counseling and commitment to change will bring you to a place of health and healing. Spend time in regular prayer and Bible reading so the Holy Spirit has the vocabulary and opportunity to speak to you about your life. Memorizing Bible verses is especially important. Find several that speak clearly of God's love and acceptance of you. One of my favorites is "In this act we see what real love is: it is not our love for God but his love for us when he sent his Son to satisfy God's anger against our sins" (1 John 4:10 TLB). Repeat them over and over when your mind is circling the drain of old lies and pain. You do not need to stay in that hard place anymore.

Your hope for peace and joy lies in God. This peace and joy do not depend on your circumstances, but on the power of God and the promises in the Bible. Our greatest promise is to go to heaven when we die, leaving all of earth's challenges and trials behind. A fear of dying need not exist for one who has faith in the One True God and all His promises. There are so many things in life worse than dying. This is not an excuse for suicide.

God has determined the number of days we will live, as the psalmist wrote, "You saw me before I was born and scheduled each day of my life before I began to breathe. Every day was recorded in your book" (Psalm 139:16 TLB). If we choose to rush our last day, we will surely miss God's best plan for us. Suicide will only stop our pain, and I believe it is the last selfish act one can do, because we think only of our own pain, not those left behind to deal with our choice. Certainly, if suicide is one of the lies you struggle with, it is time to seek professional help.

I had the wonderful experience to see a Sight and Sound Theater production in Lancaster, Pennsylvania on the life of Jesus. At one point in the play Jesus called Peter to walk to him on the Sea of Galilee. The story is found in Matthew 14:22–32. Peter left the solid wood boat, felt the water wash over his sandals, felt the wind tug on his tunic, and he set his eyes on Jesus, his Messiah.

The magnificence of overcoming the physical constraints of earth must have been wonderful. I can imagine Peter was excited to be chosen for this wonderful miracle. And then the Bible says, "He saw the wind." He took his eyes off Jesus and realized what on earth was happening. Then he sank into the sea.

As he struggled to swim in his heavy flaxen tunic, trying to gasp another breath, I can imagine he was angry. Angry at himself for believing he could pull something like this off. He may have even been angry at Jesus for calling him. He was drowning. What good was he now?

Can you hear the lies from Satan? Satan could not claim Peter's soul because Peter believed Jesus was his Messiah. But if Satan could get Peter to drown, Peter would tell no one else the good news of Jesus. Satan would have won that battle.

But Peter cried out, "Lord, save me!" Immediately, Jesus reached down through the water to grab Peter's hand and pull him to safety in the boat.

Do you understand how this story applies to your life? Whatever wind, waves, or water are surrounding you with trauma, pain, illness, or fear, they come from a sinful world full of lies and deception of Satan. They need not overcome you. Jesus will reach for you and put you on solid ground. You need only to ask, cry out, pray. He loves you. He is always with you, as Joshua wrote, "Yes, be bold and strong! Banish fear and doubt! For remember, the Lord your God is with you wherever you go" (Joshua 1:9 TLB).

If we give up our lives by suicide, only Satan wins. We are no longer able to fulfill our mission to serve God and tell others of the forgiveness of sin found in the sacrifice of Jesus. Everyone has pain and sorrow. In John 16:33 Jesus tells us to expect it because the world is full of evil. He promises we can have peace in Him because through His resurrection He overcame all the evil in the world. This is where hope lives, in the power of Jesus.

Read and Meditate

Be prepared. You're up against far more than you can handle on your own. Take all the help you can get, every weapon God has issued, so that when it's all over but the shouting you'll still be on your feet. (Ephesians 6:13 MSG)

Listen

"I Speak Jesus" by Charity Gayle
     "Promises" by Maverick City Music

As we practice the work of forgiveness we discover more and more that forgiveness and healing are one.

—AGNES SANFORD

Life lived without forgiveness becomes a prison.

—WILLIAM ARTHUR WARD

CHAPTER 11

Forgive, Not Forget

I made the forty-five–minute drive to see my Christian psychologist nearly every week during my pregnancy. I worked the evening shift in coronary and intensive care at a nearby hospital. Making time for the appointments took effort, but I was committed to becoming more emotionally stable before I gave birth. I knew postpartum depression was possible and did not want to be in the throes of a healing crisis in addition to the strain of a new baby.

I wanted to have a supervised conversation with my dad about the abuse. My counselor agreed such a conversation would do much to get me the validation I needed to move forward in my healing process. When I called Dad and asked him to attend an appointment with me, he agreed. However, when the day came, he did not arrive. My counselor called to inquire where he was and was told something came up and he would not make it. I had been quite anxious to face my dad. I was very upset to not be able to go through with the plan. I felt rejected, disrespected, and angry, an emotion I had not yet allowed myself to exhibit.

Realizing my show of anger was an important break-through, my counselor asked if I would participate in a specific counseling tool called role-playing. He explained that the two of us would sit in a room with an empty chair. I would stand before the chair and imagine my dad sitting there. I would imagine tying him to the chair with a rope so he could not leave the room. Then I would tell him all the things I had kept bottled up my entire life.

I don't remember the exact words I used to tell my "dad" how the abuse had hurt me. I wanted him to know he was wrong to use me for sex when he had a wife to fulfill his needs. He was a sick man to keep it going for so many years. He was mean to threaten to hurt me or tell others what he was doing if I did not keep the secret. He accused me of being a whore when he was the one who had turned the burning furnace of desire on in my young body.

I was especially angry that he forced me to have the abortion. I was drowning in guilt for agreeing to abort my child. The baby did not deserve to die for my sin. I could blame Dad for pushing it, but I'm the one that lay down on the surgery table. And then for him to not even accept the humanness of the fetus was another insult. I screamed and cried for many minutes, then fell weakly to the floor. So much pain, so much sorrow, such anger and hatred. I wanted to be free of it all.

I finished, weak, breathless, trying to get my crying under control. My counselor brought out a tray of communion elements and invited me to sit down with him. Before I ate the small cracker and drank the small cup of juice, we prayed together.

He prayed that God would use this session to free me of past hurt and shame. That I would accept the work of Christ's death on the cross as the payment for my sins of staying silent in the abuse and living a life of sexual promiscuity.

I confessed my complicity in the abortion. I prayed with many tears of remorse and repentance, which then turned to joy. I believed I was forgiven. I believed I was loved unconditionally by my heavenly Father. I did not need to grieve the abuse by my biological father any longer. I left that ugly experience in the pit of hell from where it originated. I did not need to grieve the death of my baby who was safely in heaven.

I will be forever grateful for the wisdom and guidance of my psychologist. I reached an important level of healing that day. I forgave myself and planned to stop carrying my guilt any longer. Even though I did not have the closure of hearing my dad apologize for the abuse, I chose to forgive him.

Many times, it was difficult to be around Dad, but with God's help I behaved in a respectful manner. If I experienced feelings of physical sickness or anxiety around him, I would leave and deal with it. At the end of his life, I was able to take leadership in his elder care and made sure he was safe and received proper medical care. Only the grace of God made my behavior possible. I did not forget what my dad had done, I forgave him for it. If I had not, my life would have been ruined by me, not him.

This is the kind of healing you can have when you trust in God to heal your pain and give you strength to behave in a healthy manner. Now I looked forward to my child's birth with more excitement and happiness than I had allowed myself to feel before. I had more confidence I would be a better parent without the emotional baggage I had carried all my life.

Read and Meditate

If you forgive those who sin against you, your heavenly Father will forgive you. But if you refuse to forgive others, your Father will not forgive your sins. (Matthew 6:14–15 NLT)

Listen

"Forgiveness" by Matthew West

"Burn the Ships" by For King and Country

It doesn't take a lot of strength to hang on.
It takes a lot of strength to let go.

—J.C. WATTS

CHAPTER 12

The Girl in the Closet

The abusive and stress–filled life I lived as a kid shaped my worldview, and I developed unique thought patterns to support it. I knew the day–to–day workings of our house and learned ways to survive within it and outside it.

An example is the way I let boys experiment with me sexually. I had learned that if you do things with people sexually, they will like you. I knew how to relate that way. I thought it was normal. But inside my spirit, it felt wrong, and I yearned to be free of the anxiety and shame. I used many behaviors and personalities to help me cope.

- Some days at school, after a night of abuse, I would be unusually quiet and avoid people.
- On other days, I would act as the class clown looking for attention and affirmation.
- Some days, I had no qualms to flirt and experiment physically with the boys.

- On other days, I would hide behind my bed to avoid the boys window-peeking on me.
- When an episode of abuse was especially bad, my mind would split. I would leave my body in the bed and my mind would go sit inside my bedroom closet. The girl inside the closet would peek out through the crack in the door waiting for the horror to end.

I was experiencing cognitive dissonance. Opposing thought processes develop in a stressful situation. You realize something is wrong, but you cannot stop it or change it. You do mental gymnastics to make all the experience fit into your mind. Your mind breaks into different compartments, and you can escape into one for help to cope with the trauma.

In her book, *Help for the Fractured Soul,* Candyce Roberts writes that many trauma survivors feel disconnected from God in spite of a deep faith. They fear if they open up to Him and ask for help, He will reveal something horrible they do not want to face.

"When a person sitting in front of you says that she wants to experience the presence of the Father, she means it; the fragments of her personality, however, do *not* want to experience the presence of God. A fragmented part of the person is generally responsible for this kind of block. A specific personality is resisting God and defending a lie."[2]

At age fourteen, I yearned to experience God's presence and drew about it on my bedroom wall. I painted one wall a

---

2   Candyce Roberts, *Help for the Fractured Soul* (Ada, Michigan: Chosen Books, 2012), 89.

beautiful royal blue color, then painted a five–foot–long white dove on it. Next to it I lettered the desire of my heart in the words of King David: "Search me, O God, and know my heart: try me, and know my thoughts: And see if there be any wicked way in me, and lead me in the way everlasting" (Psalm 139:23–24 KJV).

The wicked abuse done to me was not my responsibility, but my sexual activity was, and I was ashamed. I asked forgiveness but did not stop the sin. As long as I remained the girl in the closet and did not ask an adult to help me escape the abuse, I would not find help for my sexual addiction or my shame.

Many years later, the little girl in the closet grew up and wanted to tell the truth. I met with a Christian psychologist. My counselor showed me an illustration on his office white board. He drew a cemetery with several tombstones scattered about. Under each tombstone was a casket.

The cemetery was my life, the tombstones marked life events, and each casket was a memory. I would need to open the casket and face what was inside. I would need to do the hard work if I wanted to be free of whatever hold the memory had over me.

I am grateful that my counselor recognized I was protecting myself with several personality fragments. He reassured me that whatever the casket held, he would not judge me, he would believe me, and he would pray with me to reconcile the memory in my mind. It would no longer have a hold over me.

It took me a couple weeks of prayer and self-talk to raise up the courage to go back to the counselor and admit I wanted to see the truth. I had lived through the experiences the first time; I would survive the memory of them again.

That day we opened several caskets. The memories were dark, ugly, twisted, sorrowful. It took many tears and loud cries of hatred and pleas for mercy to work through the ordeal. I cried out to God to stop the power the abuse had over my mind. I prayed for forgiveness for all my sins, especially the sexual behaviors.

But eventually, I became quiet and was grinning from ear to ear. I had faced up to my past and had conquered several painful pieces of it. I was proud of myself. I was brave. I was strong. I was forgiven. And I had a new measure of joy.

The girl could finally come out of the closet. She was safe.

Once again, it was by the grace and mercy of God I did not give up on obeying God and kept praying for strength to heal and change. There were many consequences to my abuse and my sin. God was grieved by my sin and the pain it caused me. But He never stopped loving me. I believe, as Corrie ten Boom did, that "there is no pit of evil so deep that God's love is not deeper still."

> This High Priest of ours understands our weaknesses since he had the same temptations we do, though he never once gave way to them and sinned. So let us come boldly to the very throne of God and stay there to receive his mercy and to find grace to help us in our times of need. (Hebrews 4:15–16 TLB)

Read and Meditate

Count yourself lucky, how happy you must be—
 you get a fresh start,
 your slate's wiped clean.

Count yourself lucky—
     God holds nothing against you
     and you're holding nothing back from him.

When I kept it all inside,
     my bones turned to powder,
     my words became daylong groans.

The pressure never let up;
     all the juices of my life dried up.

Then I let it all out;
     I said, "I'll come clean about my failures to God."

Suddenly the pressure was gone—
     my guilt dissolved,
     my sin disappeared.

These things add up. Every one of us needs to pray;
     when all hell breaks loose and the dam bursts
     we'll be on high ground, untouched. (Psalm 32:1–6 MSG)

Listen
"Word of God Speak" by Mercy Me
     "There Was Jesus" by Zach Williams and Dolly Parton

If anybody understands God's ardor for His children, it's someone who has rescued an orphan from despair, for that is what God has done for us. God has adopted you. God sought you, found you, signed the papers and took you home.

—MAX LUCADO

CHAPTER 13

Grooming

The sexual use of children like me by adults creates a feeling of unease, anxiety, shame, and a sense that something is not right. Our conscience sets off an inner radar when we feel we are in a bad situation. Something is wrong. The adults are lying to us. And usually, they cause physical pain as well.

All these reactions and others are inherent in the human heart and mind because God has designed us for one pure sexual experience with a person of opposite sex and of appropriate age while married. He told us to avoid sexual experiences outside the marriage vow and bed because He knew any other sexual experience would burden us with sorrow and shame. He does not mean for us to miss out on the pleasure of sex. He wants to protect us from its wrong use.

These negative vibes that children experience during sexual experimentation or sexual abuse cause the abuser to look for ways to get around the inherent feelings. These techniques are called grooming and it means the abuser will show or do sexual things to the child to "warm them up" to cooperate.

Here are some examples of what I experienced.

I was a cute, olive–skinned, curly brown–haired and brown–eyed toddler. I liked music and could sing and dance in a way that adults found entertaining. My favorite artist was Elvis Presley. When my dad had men visit our home, he would stand me on the living room coffee table, turn on a vinyl record, and tell me to dance and sing. Of course, I loved the attention. I was a little kid. Apparently, the behavior aroused my dad, because he would set me on his lap and rub me against his body for his own pleasure. He held me tightly if I tried to wriggle away.

When I was sick with a cough or cold, he would rub Vicks VapoRub ointment on my little chest paying special attention to my tiny nipples.

I had a favorite teddy bear, probably fifteen inches tall. Dad rubbed it against my body teaching me how to masturbate.

In elementary school, I was told to straighten up the clothes in my parent's dresser. I found a pornographic magazine and took it to my mom. She threw it at my dad and told me to finish the job. Later that night, Dad brought the magazine to my room and used my hands to imitate some of the photos. I would pull away and say stop. He would cover my mouth and tell me to shush.

Once my family took a twenty–hour car trip. We stopped only for fuel. We three kids slept on the back seat, window, and floor of the car. Mom slept most of the time on car trips. We joked none of us could stand listening to the twangy country western music on the radio. I grew to hate it all, except Charlie Pride.

Dad did not trust Mom to drive so he had a hard time staying awake for those long hours. In the middle of the night, he realized I had awakened.

"Come up here and help me drive and stay awake."

As a ten–year–old kid I thought that sounded exciting. Once he had me positioned on his lap and my hands on the wheel, he began to fondle me. If I tried to push his hands away, the car would swerve and he snapped, "Watch the road!"

I was trapped. I did not want to wake my family; we were all tired from the long trip. I cried quietly and waited for him to be satisfied.

"Get back there," he sneered, as he pushed me off his lap.

What did I do wrong? I said in my mind. I was confused. I let him do what he wanted although it hurt and made me feel sick. Yet, now he acted angry, as if it was my fault.

This confusion is a powerful weapon of an abuser. It goes right along with the threats to hurt me worse if I tell others about the abuse. Promises of gifts or food treats are used as lures to get children alone when abuse can take place.

The horrible part of grooming is the abused child begins to experience the physical response God designed into our bodies for producing children and developing intimacy in a marriage. Of course, there is part pleasure in the arousal; it's a normal, physical response. Yet, this response causes terrible sadness and confusion in a child. In our mind, we know we absolutely should not be enjoying this abusive behavior, and yet the involuntary response occurs. And the abuser will use the involuntary response to prove the child "wants it" to justify their perverted use of an uncooperative victim.

Go back through the above grooming examples and look at the confusing behaviors that occurred. With any good experience came a bad one.

- Dancing for the men brought positive attention and sexual abuse
- Being comforted while sick twisted into abuse
- Having a favorite toy was tainted by inappropriate sexual behavior
- Given opportunity for the fun, grown–up experience to steer a car became a sexual encounter

This back and forth in my life scarred me for decades. If any good thing happened, I felt nervous anticipation for the bad that would follow. With the emotional problems I had, it did not take long for the bad to show up.

My emotional conflict came to be depicted in a picture. Throughout my childhood, a large picture of Jesus the Good Shepherd hung on the wall of my bedroom. It was a traditional pastoral scene, with a small brook in the background and a herd of white sheep grazing in the green pasture under a bright blue sky. Jesus stood in the center of all the beauty holding a small lamb in His arms, His expression one of peace and love.

I knew instinctively that Jesus was offering me the same comfort and care the lamb received. I believed Jesus was the Son of God who had great power and might, all knowledge and understanding, able to meet all my physical needs, and recognized my emotional pain. I believed He could see me and was interested in all I did.

Oppositely, I was ashamed and saddened to know He was watching when the wrong kind of sexual behavior went on. I did not think He was mad or would punish me. I knew He was sad about my abuse. The Bible even gives us Jesus' opinion of people who hur8t children. In Matthew 18:5 Jesus said it was better for a heavy weight to be tied around their neck and they be dropped into the sea to drown. I believed my abuser would eventually be punished.

Again, I felt the positive aspects of God's love and care, while at the same time feeling shame and sorrow at disappointing Him. Because I would not tell a grown-up about the abuse, I did not have an adult mind to help me process my confusion and speak truth into my mind.

Yet, it was my belief that kept me strong enough to function successfully outside my home. My faith carried me through to adulthood until I could get the help I needed to heal from the many years of abuse and my subsequent sinful lifestyle of promiscuous sex.

Read and Meditate

Jesus said, "Let the little children come to me and do not hinder them, for to such belongs the kingdom of heaven." (Matthew 19:14 ESV)

Listen

"Rescue" by Lauren Daigle

"I Will Wait for You (Psalm 130)" by Keith & Kristyn Getty

Spend time with Jesus Christ and allow Him to eradicate your labels and flood you with boldness and confidence—cultivating your character to move with confidence in your skills and gifts.

—Tez Brooks

CHAPTER 14

Only Two Sexes

The Bible is clear on the beginning of humanity: "So God created human beings in His own image. In the image of God he created them; male and female he created them" (Genesis 1:27 NLT). God created only two genders, male and female. That does not change with personal feelings or societal norms. It is child abuse to agree with a child's desire to be identified as other than their biological sex. The current push for explicit sex education from age three to thirteen is a method of grooming. The intention is to convince a child to accept an unhealthy thought or action regarding sexual behavior. The children are being desensitized to aberrant behavior.

For just a moment, consider the current campaign to include explicit sexual education in elementary schools regarding the LGBTQ culture. These materials could easily lead to an interest in pornographic websites. This viewing can become addictive very quickly with dire results. A steady diet of the depiction of multiple partners, bondage, and other actions can easily entice a person to force someone to imitate with them, even to the point of rape. We do not need more abusers.

Paul Batura explains it this way. "Indeed, though memories might fade, we cannot "unsee" something – especially when it comes to the formative years of childhood. Scientists confirm that young brains are far more malleable than those of adults – even likening them to Play-Doh. What we see and hear as children matters more than most people acknowledge."[3]

Sexual matters are safest when taught by a family member who understands the child's temperament, and at an appropriate age level. The radar I spoke of earlier goes off when a child sees sexual positions or same–sex relationships in a romantic sense. It happened to me when I found the porno magazine in my dad's dresser drawer. This is the God–ordained conscience to help warn of danger. The natural modesty between the sexes that protects from premarital sex is shredded. Some children cannot tolerate topics they find upsetting or offensive. It affects the rest of their studies. If the illustrations depict children in sexual context, you have now added peer pressure to a child's decision-making. No child wants to be left out of the group, including to choose a different gender if several kids around them are doing it.

Adults are to guide and instruct children, not support and promote their confusion or need for negative attention. It is wrong and harmful. It will not work in the real world, as demonstrated in recent sexual assaults by transgender males acting out

---

3 Paul Batura, "Beware the Images Culture is Placing on the Minds of Our Children," Daily Citizen, March 8, 2022, https:// dailycitizen.focusonthefamily.com/beware-the-images-culture-is-placing-on-the-minds-of-our-children/.

on biological females. God's design of sexuality wins every time. Abuse of others for our own pleasure brings pain every time.

Because of the sexual abuse I experienced, I tried to act like a boy hoping the abuse would stop. Had I lived in this current age, my desire to be a boy would have been supported. What a terrible price I would have paid had I moved into a male role, even into lesbianism. I am grateful that did not happen. The policies in schools to support children who change sexual identities is wrong. Children do not have the knowledge or experience to understand human sexuality. Guide them into better understanding. Do not encourage them to deny what God has made them to be. His plan and commandments are healthy and true. Find out what is at the root of their sexual confusion. Perhaps it is sexual abuse.

Most of the gender self-identification going on today is a disguise to participate in various sexual encounters. Once you replace a monogamous relationship between man and woman with any other, there is no limit to what kinds of activity would be practiced. It is sure to bring emptiness and sorrow, disease, and despair. Dr. James Dobson writes in the book *Children at Risk*, ". . . stability in society is dependent on the healthy expression of our sexual nature. If this energy within us is siphoned off in the pursuit of pleasure; if it is squandered in non-exclusive relations; if it is perverted in same–sex activities, then the culture is deprived of the working, saving, sacrificing, caring, building, growing, reproducing units known as families."[4]

---

4   James C. Dobson and Gary L. Bauer, *Children at Risk: The Battle for the Hearts and Minds of Our Kids* (Nashville: Thomas Nelson, Inc., 1990), 55.

If celibacy was practiced in every other relationship outside of marriage, our culture would be less broken and depraved. Once people do not control their sexual urges, other personal restraint will not occur. I know, because I lived with sexual addiction for fifteen years, and it is a terrible price to pay.

Please investigate what a belief in Jesus Christ will do to transform your desires. You can be delivered from destructive relationships. Psychological counseling can investigate the root of your desire to be other than what God created you to be. He does not make mistakes. He has a meaningful plan for your life and has the power to help you achieve it.

Read and Meditate

This is too glorious, too wonderful to believe! I can never be lost to your Spirit! I can *never* get away from my God! If I go up to heaven, you are there; if I go down to the place of the dead, you are there. (Psalm 139:6–8 TLB)

Listen

"You Say" by Lauren Daigle

"Glorious Day" by Casting Crowns

Being a believer doesn't give you immunity from the assaults of the enemy, but it does give you access to the power of the Father.

—Priscilla Shirer

CHAPTER 15

Jesus Most Powerful

The most heartbreaking side effect of child sexual abuse, in my opinion, is the deep shame and guilt that occurs in a child's heart and mind. Even though the sexual activity may start at such a young age the child is not even able to verbalize words to describe the body parts being assaulted, or even explain to someone the pain and discomfort that results, the feelings are very strong.

God designed sex to be pure in a marriage relationship. Child sexual abuse is not what God intended. Our bodies and psyches respond in the negative. We feel dirty, used up, taken advantage of, disrespected, and betrayed. Betrayal is especially deep if our abuser is a trusted relative or friend. The mixed messages from their behavior, one to provide for our needs and love us, the other to hurt us physically and confuse us emotionally and mentally, bring feelings of anger. Anger at the abuser for our suffering, anger at God for allowing the suffering.

But Jesus Himself told us to expect to suffer in this world where Satan currently has great power: "I have told you all this so that you will have peace of heart and mind. Here on earth you will have many trials and sorrows; but cheer up, for I have overcome the world" (John 16:33 TLB).

Let's look at Mark 5:1–20 for a moment. Jesus and His disciples had gone to an area called Gesera. Here was a small village on the coast of the Sea of Galilee inhabited by non-Jewish people called Gentiles. This area had not heard of Jesus' healings, miracles, and teaching about the kingdom of God. So, when Jesus encountered a man with a legion of demons inhabiting his body, the locals were not paying attention. But the demons were.

As Jesus approached the man, the demons cried out, "Jesus, Son of the Most High God, do not torment me. Do not send us out of this country but send us into that herd of pigs."

Jesus learned the demon's name was Legion "for there were many." We don't know for sure if the word *legion* meant a Roman garrison of 6,000 soldiers, or simply a very large number of demons. Regardless, no number of demons was a match for the one true Son of God. As per Satan's usual tactics, the demons felt they could escape God's judgment by striking a deal with Jesus to send them to live inside the pigs.

But as usual in God's plan, Jesus sent the demon–possessed pigs rushing down the steep bank into the sea, and they drowned. God will always conquer Satan and his demons.

Before you dismiss this event as a silly story, consider this archaeological information. The ancient village of Gerasa is modern–day Khersa in Israel. About one mile south of Khersa is a steep slope within forty yards of the shore of the Sea of

Galilee. About two miles from there are cavern tombs that appear to have been used as dwellings. These facts fit the events of the demonic healing in chapter five of Mark. I have faith the Bible is true. These facts, however, should add to your understanding.

Yes, it is Satan's power and influence that tempts people to abuse children. And yes, we children suffer under the abuse, often praying for God's deliverance from this demonic activity.

We do not understand why God does not stop the abuse. But we can always believe that God is more powerful than our abuser and He will help us through the suffering. We may not be delivered until we tell someone about the abuse, or we grow to adulthood and seek counseling to aid in our healing. But if we will call on the powerful name of Jesus, He will always be with us and help. Our hope is sure in God's power.

When we trust Christ as savior, we become children of the Most High God. He has created us to have a relationship with Him. We are esteemed and loved, precious in His sight. We need not believe the lies our guilt and shame tell us. God knows all that. He will not force His will on us but waits for us to have a loving relationship with Him as our Abba, the Aramaic word for Daddy. One who will never use us or abuse us.

Read and Meditate

For all who are led by the Spirit of God are children of God. So you have not received a spirit that makes you fearful slaves. Instead, you received God's Spirit when he adopted you as his own children. Now we call him, "Abba, Father." (Romans 8:14–15 NLT)

Listen

"Same Power" by Jeremy Camp

"What a Beautiful Name" by Hillsong Worship

Earth has no sorrow that heaven cannot heal.

—Thomas Moore

CHAPTER 16

Meeting Timmy

I lived the first five years of my life in Charleston, West Virginia. Our tract home in Orchard Manor was situated on a street of look–alike houses built for lower income families such as miners and factory workers.

The Union Carbide chemical plant could be seen at the back of a large empty field the neighborhood kids used as a play lot. We did not have lawns and yards around our houses, so we spent most of our days in the field.

One summer afternoon, several of us were playing tag when a large explosion occurred. A plume of dark smoke was emanating from the chemical plant. I learned later that several workers died, and the effects on me would last forever.

A red acid rain spilled down on us kids, burning our skin, causing us difficulty breathing. We ran around screaming which attracted the attention of the adults nearby. We were transported to the hospital for treatment. I recovered from the acute burns, inside and outside my body, but my sensitivity to petroleum chemicals was established and would affect me for the rest of my life.

Agriculture chemicals used for fertilizer and weed and pest control are petrochemicals, also called heavy metals. Many have a phosphate base that weakens muscle, specifically in my case, my heart. All have a toxic effect on the body, especially the liver and kidneys where the heavy metals are detoxified.

When we married in December 1975, my husband worked in the family farm corporation. From the time I moved to the family farm in March of 1976, I began to experience health problems—including muscle weakness, seizures, and fatigue—from sensitivity to farm chemicals.

I would spend a few weeks each winter in natural health care centers taking treatment to detoxify the heavy metals. During one of these absences, I experienced a vision that helped me heal from the abortion of my son.

The year was 1993. In the treatment center, a nurse sat with me as she monitored the intravenous solution I was receiving to flush the toxins from my system. She struck up what I'm sure she intended to be a nonchalant conversation about my children.

Unknown to her, because of the decline in my health, I was afraid I might die soon. With this on my mind, I prayed, telling God I wanted to die with a clear conscience knowing my aborted child was waiting in heaven for me.

I prayed to find a good time to speak to my teenage daughter and son about the abortion. If I survived this bout of toxicity, I wanted to volunteer at our local crisis pregnancy center. I assumed I would want to share my abortion experience with other pregnant women considering their options. I did not want to talk to strangers about my history before my children knew the truth.

"How many children do you have?" the nurse asked.

"I have two at home," I answered guardedly. My aborted child was heavy on my mind, yet I did not count him as my third child.

"You must have good help at home to care for them while you are gone."

"Yes, if not for my mother-in-law, I would probably have lost custody of my children years ago. I have a very difficult time providing for their needs."

"Mothers have a great responsibility to their children, don't we? It can be overwhelming, especially if we are sick."

And then I began to sob. As a teenager, I had relinquished my responsibility to my unborn son. I was wrong. I had enough maturity then to know I had choices and options to preserve his life. He did not have any resources except me, and I let him die. The shame, remorse, and grief washed over me.

After establishing why I was suddenly sobbing, the therapist gave me a mild sedative and asked me to try and sleep. She promised she would have a counselor come talk to me in an hour.

But God, my heavenly Father and wisest counselor of all, brought a solution to my grief I never imagined.

Surprisingly, sleep came easily. And I dreamed.

My room filled with light. The ceiling pulled back, and I saw white fluffy clouds moving across a bright blue sky, with fresh, clean air all around me. Nearby, a field of wildflowers swayed in a gentle breeze bringing their sweet fragrance toward me. The scene was calm and peaceful, and I realized I was feeling that way too. Suddenly I recognized there was a small boy, who looked to be four years old, blond, slightly built, studying a flower blossom. He stood and turned to face me. "Hi, Mommy."

I felt shocked at his greeting and at the same time, I knew him. His name was Timmy, and he was the son I had lost in my teenage abortion.

"Hi, Timmy," was all I got out before the sobs began. The shame, guilt, and grief were overwhelming. I had so much I wanted to say to him, but no words would come.

"Mommy, there is no need to feel bad anymore. You asked Jesus to forgive you years ago and He did. He does not even remember the sin of abortion anymore. He promised you that. You need to forgive yourself. I am good, Mommy. It's wonderful here. God is all I need. Please, let me go. I'll wait for you to come later, but not now."

And then, the vision was gone, and with it, much of my guilt. God answered my prayer to know Timmy was safe.

Timmy said I had asked forgiveness many years ago, and that was true. I accepted this promise: "But if we confess our sins to him,[a] he can be depended on to forgive us and to cleanse us from every wrong. And it is perfectly proper for God to do this for us because Christ died to wash away our sins*" (1 John 1:9 TLB). Timmy's reminder that God did not remember my sin was from the Bible. "He has removed our sins as far away from us as the east is from the west" (Psalm 103:12 TLB). My faith had brought me the answers I needed for further healing.

This same assurance can be yours too, dear reader. First, believe that God sent His Son Jesus to the world to make a bridge for us to have a relationship with Him. That bridge was created by the blood Jesus shed on the cross to pay for every sin of every person, past, present, or future. And His resurrection three days later provided the way for us to live in heaven when we die.

We need to confess or acknowledge that we sin. Sin is any thought, word, or action that goes against God's perfect law.

Next is repentance which means to agree with God that we have done wrong and intend to turn away from the wrong. We pray for the Holy Spirit to help us avoid the sin in the future, and we do our part to change.

Satan is the one who keeps reminding us of past sins. He knows it keeps us miserable and unable to use our spiritual gifts and abilities to serve God here on earth. If we are believers in Christ, Satan has lost his chance to keep us out of heaven when we die and spend eternity apart from God in hell. But if he can keep us feeling inadequate and unworthy of God's love and forgiveness, we miss out on the peace and joy God has planned for our lives. We will also be ineffective in sharing our faith with others and giving people an opportunity to hear the gospel and be saved.

Were I not free of the guilt of my abortion, I would not be able to speak of it with confidence and compassion. This freedom comes from my faith in Christ and my belief in the promises found in God's Word, the Bible. My hope is found in the unfailing love of God. Satan still tempts me at times with the thoughts that I am a murderer because I let the doctor take Timmy from my body. But I know God does not see me as a murderer anymore, but His cherished daughter, and I tell Satan to shut up.

One of the verses I have memorized to remind me of this unfailing love says, "For I am sure that neither death nor life, nor angels nor rulers, nor things present nor things to come, nor powers, nor height nor depth, nor anything else in all creation, will be able to separate us from the love of God in Christ Jesus our Lord" (Romans 8:38–39 ESV).

Scripture is our best weapon against Satan's lies. I rest in this assurance.

I want to tell you one more consequence of my abortion. My children received the news of my abortion with respect and understanding. Later that evening, I found my teenage son crying in his bedroom. His explanation broke my heart; he was mourning the death of his older brother.

"It would be really nice to have a brother," he said sorrowfully.

Read and Meditate

There is now no condemnation for those who are in Christ Jesus. For the law of the Spirit of life has set you free in Christ Jesus from the law of sin and death. (Romans 8:1–2 ESV)

Listen

"Mighty to Save" by Laura Story

"How Great is Our God" by Chris Tomlin

We cannot change our past. We cannot change the fact that people act in a certain way. We cannot change the inevitable. The only thing we can do is play on the one string we have, and that is our attitude.

—CHUCK SWINDOLL

Chapter 17

Embracing Joy and Purpose

I was in the middle of shopping when my cell phone vibrated. I didn't recognize the number.

I had made a habit not to pick up unknown numbers, plus my hands were full of t-shirts. I was anxious to complete my purchase and get out of town, yet I felt the Lord nudge me that this was a call I should take.

I set the shirts down on the table and began walking to the front of the store to get privacy for the call. As I reached the door, I clicked on the call button and answered.

"This is JoAnn."

"JoAnn, this is Ted[5]*, do you remember me? Mom said you would remember me if I called you. Do you?"

I did recognize the frantic voice on the line and became instantly concerned about the reason for his call. I responded in a calm voice hoping to defuse his anxiety.

---

5   * Not his real name.

"Of course! How could I forget one of the boys who stuck out my Sunday school class all through middle school! How long has that been, Ted? Are you out of college now?"

"What, yeah, college. No, I quit after three years. Things have been complicated. And now they are worse! You have to help me, please. It's a matter of life and death!"

Oh, God, please give me your words right now, I prayed silently before answering. Then I said, "Okay, Ted, let's start here. I need you to take a really deep breath, right now. I'm not kidding. Can you do that for me? Let me hear you."

And thank God, he did just that.

"Okay, one more deep one. Good. Now, start at the beginning."

"I have this girlfriend. We are not very good together. We keep breaking up and getting back together, but things don't change much."

"Is that because you are sleeping together? Is your relationship not very strong?"

"Yeah, I guess so. You told us sex would keep a relationship from growing strong and it's been true for me, but I still don't stop it."

"That's a talk for another time. Let's focus on the life-and-death problem."

"I need you to talk to my girlfriend. You have to tell her what you told us in Sunday school about abortion killing a real baby and not solving any problems. Please! She's pregnant and is scheduled for an abortion. She won't listen to me. She wants to get rid of the problem. Please tell her it won't help."

"Of course, I would be happy to talk to her, but I have a feeling she won't listen. It sounds like you do not have the leadership in this relationship, Ted. God wants you to man up and save your child."

"How do I do that? She's going tomorrow!"

"Does she claim to be a Christian?"

"Yes, but so do I," he said quietly, with shame in his voice.

"Don't do that, Ted. Don't let the shame prevent you from making good decisions. Have you prayed for forgiveness?"

"Yes."

"Then your guilt is a moot point. Let's focus on praying for the life of your child. Have you done that?"

"No," he said. "But she is such a bitch about things, I can't push back."

"Then stop pushing. Love her, respect her, tell her you believe the baby is a human and needs a father, that you will be that father. But don't promise to marry her if your relationship is this bad."

"I don't know if I can say that. I'm really scared, JoAnn."

"I know how you feel," I said. "You know I know. God is big enough for this problem. He can save that baby and you can help. Are you brave enough to face her and not just call her? You may not believe me, but she is looking for you to lead now. She may be scared too."

"No, she got pregnant on purpose. She's older than me, and she wants kids. She doesn't want marriage. That's why this abortion appointment makes no sense."

"Oh, boy, you have some big problems there. But let's focus on the baby again. Will you try to talk to her one more time? If she got pregnant on purpose, she may be jerking your chain about the abortion. She sounds like a drama queen."

"That's true," he said.

"Then let's get her to reign over a better decision and keep that baby alive. Let's pray now."

It was difficult to find the right words. I simply asked for God's will in the situation. It was far too complicated for me to solve. Ted hung up a little calmer and I heard determination in his voice to ask his girlfriend one more time to keep the baby.

I was crying after the call. I was sad to hear the story of sex, drama, lack of respect. It was the story I had lived as a teenager, and I knew how bad it felt. I did not want that for Ted. I grieved for the baby nestled in his mother's womb unaware of his impending death sentence. I pleaded with the Lord to change her mind, not just for the baby's sake, but hers too. I knew the guilt and shame of being complicit in the murder of an unborn child. I did not want her to suffer those consequences.

Lastly, I was amazed, and grateful, that God had given me the opportunity to see I had influenced Ted. He had been in seventh grade when I taught the lesson on the wrongness of elective abortion. Now, ten years later, he was having to apply it to his own life. That part felt good, to have been obedient to tell my honest story and give clear Bible teaching. That made me smile.

And thank God, I got another call the next week that the girlfriend had agreed to carry the baby to term. She and Ted would have several months to figure out their plans to co-parent their son.

Some people never recover from sexual abuse. It defines the majority of their experiences for the rest of their lives. They continue feeling as if they will always be a victim. It becomes their identity. They survive, but never thrive.

I'm living proof that it doesn't have to be that way.

God is bigger than our wounds, and He can heal us and empower us for lives filled with purpose and joy. For me, I found purpose and joy in helping others.

Teaching children about God has been a big part of my life. I helped start the children's church program when my kids were babies. As they grew, I moved up to teaching their Sunday school classes. My favorite age to teach was sixth grade. In fact, I bonded so much with the class that Ted was in that I followed those kids through middle school. We remained close through their high school graduation. A few are still close friends today.

I also had the privilege of being a volunteer leader and director for our Awana Bible club for forty years. I loved the weekly focus on Scripture memorization because I knew how much the verses I learned as a child had comforted and corrected me all my life. Since I had made the decision to accept Jesus as my savior at a young age, I knew that the kids in my Awana club had the maturity and understanding to make that decision too. It was a wonderful event every time a child responded to our Bible teaching and was led by the Holy Spirit to accept Jesus as savior.

Many gifted Christian adults served faithfully with me as leaders every week. We put in the extra effort to keep our club exciting with theme nights and award parties. I awarded two of my grandkids their Timothy trophy for completing four years in my club. They both served as junior leaders while in high school.

God also opened doors for me to host weekly women's Bible studies at my home. Leaving the teaching to women with that gift, I get to use my gift of hospitality to create a warm, welcoming environment in which women get to encounter God. The studies always help me to grow deeper in my faith and Bible knowledge, as well as develop deeper friendships with the women in the group.

As a member of our church missions committee for twenty-five years, I had many opportunities to use my skills of organization, leadership, and teaching to plan and participate in trips inside the United States and to foreign countries with other adults and teenagers.

It is exciting to tell people that the Lord helps me cope with the stresses of life and my faith brings me joy in the midst of suffering. To be able to share the gospel message with someone who has never heard is a special duty. The sufferings may be different for each one, but the One True God has answers for everyone.

There are so many needs around us, and allowing God to use me to meet those needs has been—and still is—a precious journey.

When the home of a family in our church burned to the ground, I helped them settle in temporary housing, then coordinated a campaign that raised thousands of dollars for them to begin to rebuild their lives.

Another young couple was moving to a foreign country as missionaries. I stayed awake all night helping the young mom sort through their belongings to select what they would need for the next three years away from shopping in the United States.

I don't say these things to brag on myself, but to encourage you. Whatever hardships and pain you have experienced, God has healing, joy, and purpose for you. He has given these things to me, and I know He wants you to experience them, too.

I left my nursing job in coronary and intensive care after five years due to serious health problems. I had been feeling convicted about the need to homeschool my kids, and quitting my job gave me the time to teach. We had eight wonderful years together.

Then, when my kids were teenagers, they told me my poor health was keeping them from getting the education they needed and asked to go to a public classroom. They transferred to a nearby Christian high school, graduated, and then each graduated from college.

Homeschool is a wonderful way of life that takes prayer, dedication, and patience. There is no perfect school, home, or Christian, but I believe my kids had more benefit than harm from both experiences.

After my children graduated from high school in the late nineties, I wondered if I could return to practice medicine.

I had used alternative natural health care to treat my chronic sensitivity to agriculture chemicals for several decades. One day, my personal naturopathic physician asked me to attend a new school he was organizing to teach pharmacists to be naturopaths. I was one of three women in a class of seventy men. The education was the most fulfilling three years of my life.

I developed a private practice with 150 clients in my database. Because of my own experiences with chronic illness, abuse, abortion, and sexual sins, I had great intuition into other people's problems. I gave good advice and helped people of all ages achieve better health. I thank God for the significant meaning and fulfillment it brought to my life.

Read and Meditate

For I know the plans I have for you, says the Lord. They are plans for good and not for evil, to give you a future and a hope. In those days when you pray, I will listen. You will find me when you seek me, if you look for me in earnest. (Jeremiah 29:11–13 TLB)

Listen

"Because He Lives (Official Music Video)" by Celtic Worship
  "It's About the Cross" by the Ball Brothers

CHAPTER 18

Floods of Sorrow

After being in private practice for fourteen years, I was diagnosed with cancer. The cancer development proved to be the last straw regarding my chronic illness, and I realized I could no longer remain living on our farm surrounded by agricultural crops. The toxicity would continue to harm my body. I needed to be away from the area to avoid the exposure. I purchased a small cabin in the Colorado mountains and lived there during five months of the farming season every year. My overall health improved dramatically.

The Lord provided another ministry for me as landlord to people who rented two apartments on my property. I often invited my renters to share a meal and showed interest in their lives. There were occasions when I would adjust the rent to help provide for their needs. A few times, I had to evict someone for breaking the rules of my lease but, even then, they knew I cared about them and wanted them to live better lives. They rarely left angry.

As a lifelong resident of the Midwest plains, I never dreamed I would learn to hike in Rocky Mountain National Park. But I had several wonderful friends who taught me to hike safely and to enjoy God's wonderful creation of creatures and mountains. I hosted many people at my cabin so others could enjoy the mountains too. My grandchildren visited every summer and we made wonderful memories together.

I attended a good church in Colorado and became the youngest member of the single senior ladies' social group. We enjoyed Sunday meals together. I gained important knowledge as I listened to their years of life experience and spiritual wisdom. I became friends with several who appreciated the time I spent to visit them in their homes. As each one has died and gone to be with Jesus, in my sorrow I have found comfort to know I will resume our friendship in heaven when I go.

In September 2013, I was awakened by a phone call warning me a catastrophic flood was coming through my canyon. I lived next to the Big Thompson River and was surprised and frightened to see the rushing, rising current. I saw a light on at a neighbor's cabin on the other riverbank and realized someone must have arrived overnight. The water was at my ankles when I crossed the bridge to rescue the vacationers. Ten minutes later, the water was at our knees as the two women carried their dog and a few belongings to my car. I settled them in a Red Cross motel and took their dog to the vet for boarding.

My best friend was stranded in her cabin a half mile down river. I met with authorities three times begging them to go get her. When the rescuers arrived on the second day, twenty-two people and ten dogs had gathered from her side of the mountain to get food and water at her cabin. It took seven hours to lower each one over the side of a thirty–foot mountain cliff in a wire basket. I was very relieved no one was injured in the rescue.

For a few weeks, my dog and I moved into town with friends. I went back and forth to my property, working by myself to pull the wet flooring, ruined furniture, mud, and debris from my apartments. Thank God the flood prevention I had done to the property years earlier had spared my main cabin from major damage. A neighbor used his skid steer to move the mud from my yard. The changing water table caused my water well to dry up and a new one would need to be drilled.

I was grateful for my safety and that of my best friend, but I was tired and discouraged and anxious to go home to Nebraska.

Finally, several weeks after the rains had stopped, I was able to return to my Nebraska home.

A few days later, while reviewing my credit card bill to make sure that a canceled hotel reservation had been refunded, I found a long list of unknown charges.

During my research, I saw these odd charges went back for a year.

When I questioned my husband about the matter, he said he was aware and was taking care of it. Since he was busy with harvest, I started making calls to vendors myself.

In the process, I was shocked to discover that my husband was having an affair with a scam artist. He had been embezzling from our company for over a year to support his girlfriend and trying to hide it until an anticipated windfall could be deposited in the farm account.

In October I left my home to separate from my marriage while business was tended to. The result was the deconstruction of the family corporation, and the loss of my home, job, and lifestyle.

We were separated three years during which time my husband made no effort to reconcile with me or our children. When he made it clear he would not give up his girlfriend, I filed for divorce which was granted in April 2016.

I fought off shame and embarrassment for ending a forty–year marriage that had been made as a covenant before God. I had taken my vows from the book of Ruth and had promised that his people would be my people as long as I lived.

Once again, I was not spared the turmoil of this world, but I can say that Jesus walked with me all along the way, meeting my needs at every turn. I can honestly testify that God will work all things together for good if we will follow His commands and seek righteousness.

A few months after the divorce was final, I experienced another heartbreak. An early morning phone call awakened me to catastrophic news: my best friend's daughter had died in her sleep.

I rushed to my friend's cabin. It was gut-wrenching to speak with the authorities, make phone calls, and hug her while the black bag on the gurney was wheeled out the door. Her daughter had become my good friend too. I was so sad. Our faith in God and confidence in our friendship helped us heal as we processed the grief.

All the needed repairs and remodeling to my property was completed after the flood, and I enjoyed five more years of healthy mountain living. Unfortunately, living at high elevation for ten years taxed my heart, already weakened by farm chemicals. My heart disease worsened, so I sold my cabin in 2018 and returned to living in Nebraska full time.

I prayed for God to lead me to a new ministry that would keep me off the farm during the summer, and I was directed to volunteer with Joni and Friends ministry to the disabled and their families.

Each summer I choose a state where a family retreat is scheduled. I volunteer at the camp and then remain in the area for several months, returning home after harvest is well underway. Because of my nursing and naturopath education, I am not intimidated to befriend and assist my friends with disabilities or to be a listening ear to their family members.

Like the rest of the world, the COVID chaos of 2020 brought many challenges, not the least for me was another cancer diagnosis. The malignancy and aggressive nature of the cancer cell prompted me back into cancer treatment for all of 2021.

Facing a possible end–of–life scenario made me consider what I wanted to finish before death. I remembered my desire to tell the story of my childhood abuse in hopes I could help others cope with the trauma and seek healing.

Despite being in cancer treatment, I took the leap of faith to sign a publishing contract. I was eager to go public with my memories and experiences. God granted me the blessing of cancer remission and I began to write.

God has been so good to me. Despite the deep wounds from the sexual abuse of my childhood, He has brought healing, purpose, and joy into my life.

Read and Meditate

Let me see your kindness to me in the morning, for I am trusting you. Show me where to walk, for my prayer is sincere. (Psalm 143:8 TLB)

Listen

"It is Well With My Soul" by Chris Rice
    "Find Us Faithful" by Steve Green

God feels the pulse and prescribes the medicine.

—ARABIAN PROVERB

CHAPTER 19

Flame Out

My parents had been living in a care facility for four years when I started getting calls from the care facility director.

On a Tuesday morning I found myself sitting in the director's office. We had several of these meetings over the past week, and I knew what she needed to discuss with me: she was going to give me another report of my dad's inappropriate behavior with a resident.

Dad's brain function was diminishing with age. Also disappearing were any filters that had—albeit imperfectly—kept his sexual impulses in check. Increasingly, he was harassing women residents of the facility.

The director was running late that day, and I found myself waiting in her office with a few minutes to reflect.

It's funny how memories emerge when you least expect them. I thought of the night my dad insisted on walking my sixth-grade girlfriend home from our house. I remembered the sound of her sobs when she told me later, "Your dad kissed me on the mouth! What is wrong with him?"

I thought of how I screamed at my dad, "Can't you leave *anyone* alone?"

Now, fifty years later, I had my answer, and the answer was "No."

As the director walked into the room, I could see from the look on her face I was in for another embarrassing talk. Only this time she was in no position to extend my dad any more grace.

"We have video proof of your dad's most recent encounter," she explained with a mix of sympathy and frustration. "We cannot allow your father to continue living in our facility. I realize with the acceleration of his dementia he is not legally aware and responsible for his behavior. However, I am asking you to remove your father from our facility and find him a more appropriate place to stay. Your mother is welcome to remain here, but I need your father out within twenty-four hours. In addition, until he is gone you must arrange for someone to remain here and keep him under constant supervision."

It was humiliating. I felt guilty and sorry for the women he was bothering. Staff was keeping the information from my mom to spare her the embarrassment. I would have liked to have been spared too.

I left the director's office and went to make myself comfortable in my parent's apartment. I spent several hours on the phone contacting Veterans Administration and civilian facilities looking for a place for Dad to live. Twenty-two homes turned me down as soon as they heard why I needed the placement.

A local social worker was helping me navigate the process. It was exhausting.

When it came time for bed, I placed a chair in front of my parent's bedroom door and had a déjà vu moment. As a college student home on summer break, I used to wedge a chair beneath my bedroom doorknob to keep Dad *out* and protect myself. Now I was doing it to keep him *in* and protect others.

I slept on the couch that night. Dad woke up a few times in the night and I walked him in the hallways until he could settle down and sleep again.

The next morning, I drove Dad to a nearby town and checked him into a temporary situation for safekeeping. The next day he was admitted to a psychiatric hospital 100 miles away where he stayed three weeks.

While he was in the hospital, I continued my search for suitable housing. One day I drove 250 miles to visit five facilities. At the fifth place, I had a disturbing interview with the social worker.

"You need to understand no one is going to want your dad admitted to their facility. He is a threat to our population, and we simply cannot accept him. You are going to need help to find a safe place. I'm sorry. I've seen this before and it's a very difficult time for a family."

That was certainly true for our family.

I eventually found a small care facility about thirty miles from my home that agreed to admit Dad to their drug rehab wing. This area was under constant lockdown and supervision. However, when the staff realized he was being mistreated by young addicts who were taking advantage of his weakened state, he was moved to the memory care wing where a staff member was always with him.

In a short time, the dementia advanced to the point where he behaved as a mild-mannered young child without much speech or interaction with others. Now, at last, he was safe to be in the general population. The flame had burned out. My mom moved into his facility and saw him for his final months.

My brother and sister worked full time and lived far away, so most of the day-to-day responsibility for our parents' care fell to me. With my medical background it was only natural that I be the one to speak with doctors about Dad's case and pass the information on to them. My siblings and I are blessed to share a faith in Jesus, and we usually agreed on all the decisions regarding our parents' elder care. Each one of us brought our own gifts and abilities to the problem and we worked as a team—not only to give our dad the best quality of care under the circumstances, but also to support our mom. While she and Dad lived in different facilities, she suffered loneliness and loss of control over Dad's life. My siblings' phone calls and visits were a great comfort to her.

It was weird relating to my dad those last months. He acted like a young boy and told me stories about growing up in the days before he joined the carnival. I actually enjoyed talking to him. He seemed liked a different person and I could separate this man from the one who had hurt me for so many years.

I got the call in the middle of the night that my dad had died suddenly in his sleep.

Mom's favorite nurse sat with her in Dad's room for an hour as they waited for the funeral home to receive his body.

I chose to wait until morning to go see her. My choice may be misunderstood by many, but I know I did my best for my parents and there were times I had to save myself.

Despite the fact that, in the end, I was able to separate the man-child before me from the man who had abused me, the history of abuse from Dad made everything about his deterioration difficult.

It was embarrassing to watch video of my dad being inappropriate with other people. I felt like I had to take care of this monster when all I wanted to do was curl on the floor, close my eyes, plug my ears, and say "nananana" until the crazy quit. I had to pray every day during every appointment, and in every car ride with Dad, that I would remain calm and respectful. I wanted to fulfill my responsibility as his daughter and get Dad the care he needed. It was very hard.

You must believe me when I say there is no way on earth that I could have handled this stage of my dad's life without my faith in God. God gave me strength and wisdom. In every circumstance, God provided guidance I needed from doctors, nurses, and other staff members who understood what I was up against. I kept telling myself, *This isn't their first rodeo. They are not judging you for the actions of your father. You can do this, just take it one day at a time.*

Two of my friends had been through the end–of–life stage with their parents and I talked to them a lot. My pastor was a big support too.

By the time of his death, I was no longer my dad's victim. In Christ, I had become a victor. I was safe. And I had—with God's help—navigated a whole new set of experiences that might, one day, help me help others in their journeys from abuse to victory.

As I reached my sixty-third birthday, little did I know that I had one more important lesson to learn.

Read and Meditate
O Lord, don't hold back your tender mercies from me! My only hope is in your love and faithfulness. (Psalm 40:11 TLB)

Listen
"The Steadfast Love of the Lord Never Ceases" by Maranatha Singers
"Cast My Cares" by Shane and Shane

CHAPTER 20

JoAnn with a Capital A

When I turned sixty-three, I applied for Social Security benefits. It seemed like a simple enough process. Little did I know
God would use this experience to bring one more layer of
healing to my life.

Before I tell you what happened, I must tell you about
something I discovered as a child that haunted me for decades.

With the normal curiosity of any young child, I often got
into things in our house that were off limits. One of the things
I was most curious about was a locked green metal storage box,
like a fishing tackle box, stored in a closet.

I knew where the key was kept and, on several occasions,
snuck open the box and explored the contents. Among the
pieces of jewelry my mom brought from Lebanon were several
important legal documents and a letter.

Why I opened the letter and read it will remain a mys-
tery to me, but information it contained added to my loss of
self-worth.

The letter was written by a psychiatrist who saw my mom in a hospital. I do not know the reason for her admission, but I would assume it had something to do with mental health, or lack thereof. In the letter, the doctor said my mom was pregnant. She was sick from the abusive relationship with her husband, and she did not want to have the baby.

That was me.

I was born in 1955 after twenty-four hours of difficult labor. In those days, women were confined to the hospital for a week after giving birth. During the week, Mom wanted to name me after her foster sister but could not think of a middle name.

The family story goes that each day the maternity nurse on duty would ask my dad for a name for my birth certificate. Each time he would say they had not chosen a middle name yet. At the end of the week as my mom and I were being wheeled down the hall, the nurse hollered, "What is the baby's name?"

"I don't know," my dad answered. "You name her."

Throughout my young life, my parents told me they had not been able to choose a middle name they liked. They told me the first name box on my birth certificate read Jo Ann, and the middle name box was blank.

It would seem innocent enough, but it caused me a lifetime of angst and confusion.

I resented the nicknames. Jo, JoJo, or the worst, JoJo from Kokomo. With the advent of computers, having a space between Jo and Ann made for more confusion. A computer would not recognize the capital A, nor would it accept the space. Instead, my name was usually recorded as Jo. I hated it!

I yearned for a middle name. The elementary children around me had middle names. The Catholic kids even had two, one being their confirmation name. I would sit at my school desk, writing with my number two pencil on my Big Chief tablet, and practice my ideas for a middle name. Marie was my favorite. I never told anyone this part of my story.

I was seventeen years old when I applied for college and had to order a copy of my legal birth certificate. I was horrified to read my first name was Jo and my middle name was Ann. Apparently the nurse had made her decision. My name was Jo. Nevertheless, I refused to acknowledge the truth. I continued to record my legal name as Jo Ann with no middle name.

Many years passed and although I had experienced much emotional healing, the legal spelling of my name still made me angry.

I believe God is aware of every detail in my life no matter how minor or small it may seem. I soon learned God had a plan to help me with my name problem when I applied for Social Security benefits at age sixty-three. I filled out the paperwork just as I had for my driver's license, marriage license, and passport: Jo Ann, no middle name. And a couple weeks later, the phone rang.

A government employee from Social Security in Kansas was calling to ask me to explain why I was committing identity theft. Unfortunately, my response was to laugh.

And her response was to find nothing funny about the call. The government did not have a Social Security number for me and would not allow me to apply for benefits. I immediately sobered my tone and said, "May I tell you a short story?" And she listened to my tale.

When I concluded, the line was quiet for several seconds. I waited anxiously wondering what she was thinking.

When she spoke, her voice was calm and respectful.

"I believe what you are telling me, and I'm sorry you have struggled with the spelling of your name for so long. However, according to the United States government, your name is Jo. If you want any benefits, you will direct me to change your name in your paperwork and proceed. I suggest if you are unhappy, you contact an attorney and change your name in court. Good day."

For the next two years, my mail was addressed to Jo. All the charities and businesses picked up on the change. Every day mail arrived addressed to Jo. And every day, I felt angry!

Of course, no one close to me was aware of this scenario. I continued to call myself Jo Ann. But it wasn't enough. I hated my name. And then it hit me. Why did I hate it so much? I had to understand. I called my psychologist and asked for a meeting.

I wasn't two minutes into reciting the story before she interrupted me. And if you know anything about professional counseling, counselors do not usually interrupt. She caught my attention.

"Why don't you change your name?" my doctor asked, quite matter-of-factly. In fact, so matter-of-factly, it did not compute.

"What did you say?" I asked quizzically.

"Why don't you change your name? Call yourself anything you want. It's not a difficult thing to do. People do it every day. You need an attorney, and you need to speak to a judge. It will cost some money. Just do it. Be who you want to be. Isn't it about time? Your dad did not respect you enough to name you.

That disrespect continued with the chronic abuse. You have an opportunity to change."

It was a short session. As soon as I arrived home, I called my attorney and asked for an explanation of what it would take to legally change my name. Of course, he was confused. I had divorced four years earlier and made the decision to not take back my maiden name. He assumed that was the change I wanted to make.

"No, I want a middle name."

"What does that mean, a middle name? Your name is Ann."

"Yes, I realize that, but it has never been who I am. I am Jo Ann. Now I want to be JoAnn Marie. I want the letter A in JoAnn to be capitalized, with no space. I want it to be a visible reminder that I stood up to my dad and took control of who I would be."

"We will start work on it right away. It will be good to see you again, JoAnn Marie."

The smile in his voice was matched by the grin on my face and my fist in the air. Courage at any time will get you results in healing, even at age sixty-five.

Realizing the role disrespect played in my child abuse was an important part of healing. Once again, God used Christian counseling to open my eyes to feelings I could not sort out on my own.

I am very thankful for the godly counselors God put in my life. The guidance and advice from a biblical perspective kept me grounded in eternal truth and promise. Whatever earthly distress I encountered, my knowledge of heavenly truth fought and won the battle for my mind. By faith, I believed God loved me. He had created me and knew my name. Whatever man thought of or did to me would not change this truth.

The television show *The Chosen* had a beautiful episode depicting Mary Magdalene being redeemed by Jesus from her years of demonic possession. My tears flowed freely to hear Jesus say these sweet words of acceptance to her:

But now thus says the Lord, He who created you, O Jacob, He who formed you, O Israel:

> "Fear not, for I have redeemed you; *I have called you by name, you are mine.*
> When you pass through the waters, I will be with you;
>   and through the rivers, they shall not overwhelm you;
> when you walk through fire you shall not be burned,
>   and the flame shall not consume you."
>
> (Isaiah 43:1–2 ESV)

Even the burning fire of child sexual abuse cannot consume one safely in God's care.

Listen

"In Christ Alone" by Keith & Kristyn Getty and Alison Krauss
    "God and God Alone" by Steve Green

AFTERWORD

I suffered through the difficult memories and ugly subject matter of incest to write my story because I want you to find healing. Whether your abuse was incest, rape, prostitution, sex slavery, or any other sexual abuse, you can find health, healing, and forgiveness toward yourself and your abuser.

The confusion, guilt, shame, and personal regret that resulted from chronic childhood sexual abuse was devastating. I simply did not understand what was happening to me and what dysfunction and depravity it established in my mind and body. I often thought my only escape was through death at my own hand.

Due to the early sexualization of my psyche by the sexual abuse, I spent fifteen years in the dysfunction of sexual addiction. If not for the intervention of God in my life through the work of the Holy Spirit, I would not have escaped that sin.

I am talking about my experience with child sexual abuse, and recovery from it, because I want you to have a voice in your own recovery. I want you to gain the vocabulary to express yourself. I want you to realize you are not the only person hurt this way. Tragically, child sexual abuse is very common, and more so today. You are not alone.

You have never been alone. Whether you have a personal faith in God or not, God has been, is now, and always will be, with you. He is aware of your struggles. It may not be His will to interfere to stop the struggle, but He promises He will be with you in it. It will gain you nothing to be angry at God because He allowed the abuse. We cannot understand God's mind. If we did, He would not be God. But we can trust He wants only good things for us. We can have faith He has everything under control even though we suffer. This world is evil. God is good, and heaven is real and perfect. We can go there someday. I hope to meet you there.

As I have testified repeatedly, faith in God and living life through the power of the Holy Spirit is where true, complete healing comes from. First, if you trust in Christ as your savior, you will find forgiveness for all your sin. Then, as you study the Bible and pray for God's help, you will learn the truth you need to combat the lies Satan puts in your mind. At the time you believe, you become a new creation; all the old harmful, hurtful ways of your life are gone. The Bible will teach you how you can start over and experience loving, respectful relationships.

It will take work. You will need to admit you have a problem. You will need to stop the victim thinking and turn to restorative thinking. I strongly urge you to find a Christian counselor for regular talk sessions and the EMDR therapy I mentioned earlier.

It will take time, maybe a long time. Do not be discouraged if the process is slow or when you find yourself repeating unhealthy thoughts and actions. Admit you are doing it, pray for forgiveness, ask God for help and strength to begin anew. You can do this. If God is for you, none can be against you.

God bless you in your journey. If you want to talk to me about anything, contact me at my web site, JoAnnMarieSpeaks. com

A Letter to My Readers

Dear reader,

If you have gotten to this page in my book, you may be asking yourself, *Is she ever going to stop talking?* And yet I believe you have come to this page for a special purpose. I want to talk to you one last time about my belief that my faith in God helped me survive and heal from my sexual abuse, and why I have thrived in spite of life's many struggles and trials.

At the beginning of my story you read the questions I asked while hiding in a cellar:

- Why don't grownups recognize my trouble?
- Why don't I tell someone?
- Why isn't God answering my prayer of deliverance?

I was six years old in that cellar and did not have the maturity or life experience to answer the first two. But I knew God was hearing my prayer even if I was not getting the answer I wanted. I believed God loved me and had the power to help me. If I had told a trusted adult about my abuse, God would have used them to deliver me. But I didn't. That's on me, not God.

A year later when I prayed to receive Jesus Christ as my personal savior, I began my faith journey. I have learned about God through His Word, the Bible, His guidance in my life, and through answered prayer. It is important you know what my faith is based on.

I believe in the One True God who:

- Created everything in the universe: earth, planets, sun, stars, galaxies, all of it.
- Created everything in and on the earth: humans, mammals, reptiles, plants, minerals, air, and water, all that we experience.
- Created humankind in His image which means we think, relate, create, feel, understand.
- Gave us free will. He allows us to think for ourselves, behave according to our thinking, and accept the consequences for our actions. In the 1970s we had a quote something like: "If you love someone, let them go. If they don't come back, they were never really yours." God loves us enough to let us go our own way, but He wants us to live in obedience to His ways. We will suffer consequences if we don't.
- Has a character that is all-knowing, loving, merciful, patient, persistent, strong, truthful, and faithful. Unlike us, He can *never* be untrue to His character— He is who He is.
- Has a master plan for our individual lives and the lives and workings of the whole world.

- Sent His Son Jesus Christ to earth, whose death and resurrection is the only way to eternal life.

Now, ask me: "If God is 'God,' why does He allow bad things to happen?"

It is an important question, but the answer is hard to understand. God does not *make* bad things happen. His love for us makes that impossible. He does allow people to use their free will to do bad things with terrible consequences. Everything you and I have gone through has been some of those consequences. Our abuser acted from the sinful nature of every man since Adam and Eve. They chose to do evil things.

God wants us to choose Him. But unlike your abuser, He will not force you into anything.

Despite the childhood abuse and other difficult experiences of my life, I always chose God. I believed the same God who created the universe created me. He loves me. He never abandoned me while I was going through horrible things. My faith brought the good results of courage, hope, patience, independence, empathy for the suffering of others, and a greater dependence on God. I want you to know that good can come out of the bad times. It can happen for you too.

The subtitle of my book says I have moved from victim to victor. A victim is someone who chooses to live in the past, allowing it to take away their right to choose a different future. God wants you to choose to turn to Him for strength to forgive, to heal, to help others, to change your life completely. Simple, individual choices can give us freedom. From this point forward, it is your choices that will define you.

Please consider once more what changes a personal relationship with Jesus Christ can bring about in your life. God has a wonderful plan for your life. He wants you to know Him now and have you spend eternity with Him in heaven after you die.

First, we must understand we all sin: we think, do, or say things that do not please God. This sin separates us from God, and we cannot enter heaven. There is nothing we do in our own effort that will cover this sin problem: not being good, doing good, religious rituals, or anything else.

God sent His Son Jesus to cover our sin problem. He lived a perfect life, died on a cross, was raised from the dead after three days, and lives in heaven. It is only the perfect blood sacrifice of His death on the cross that paid for our sins. And it is because of God's love for us that He provided this plan so we could have a personal relationship with Him.

While Jesus was on earth, He said He could answer prayer, forgive sin, judge the world, and give us eternal life, and He did countless miracles to back up His claims. We need only accept Jesus' love and sacrifice for us to attain all these promises.

We accept Jesus by faith. We can do nothing to earn it. We believe that Jesus is the Son of God. We invite Him to guide and direct our lives.

You can receive Jesus Christ right now. You do not need to say a specific prayer because God knows what is in your heart. He understands what you want to do. It is not the prayer that saves you. But if it will help you be more comfortable, here is an example of what you might say to God right now.

Jesus, I am a sinner and I want to live differently. I am sorry for my sinful life. I believe you died on the cross to pay for my sin. I believe you came back from the dead making the way for me to live in heaven for all eternity. I accept this free gift of forgiveness. Please give me the power to change and become the person you created me to be. Amen.

Now that you are a follower of Jesus Christ, a Christian, here is some information to help you begin your faith walk with Jesus.

Learn more about God through Bible reading and prayer.
- Do not be confused because the Bible has been rewritten in many modern translations. Most of them are safe and accurate. Throughout my book I often used one called *The Living Bible* to make the verses easier to read. Another good study Bible is the English Standard Version.
- Whichever version you choose, ask God to help you understand what you read, then live what you learn.

Attend a church that teaches from the entire Bible.
- Attend regularly.
- Ask the leaders how you can be involved in church activities. You have unique gifts and abilities that will make you an important part of the church congregation.
- Introduce yourself to people and make friends. Don't sit back and wait for others to be your friend. This is how a victim behaves. Now you are a Christian. You have victory over sin and past habits in your life. People will accept you.

Stay away from people in your old lifestyle until you are healthier and have learned more about God's ways. Then you will be better able to resist the temptation to go back to it. When you are around them, show them God's love, and they will see the changes He has made in your life.

Remember, if you fall back into old ways, stop quickly, confess it to God, ask for His strength to start new again. God loves you and wants the very best in life for you. He will help you.

I pray God will open your mind and heart to His truth in these Bible verses. Complete healing can be yours through faith in Christ.

Jeremiah 29:11–13 (TLB) For I know the plans I have for you, says the Lord. They are plans for good and not for evil, to give you a future and a hope. In those days when you pray, I will listen. You will find Me when you seek Me, if you look for Me in earnest.

Isaiah 53:6 (TLB) *We*—every one of us—have strayed away like sheep! *We,* who left God's paths to follow our own. Yet God laid on *him* the guilt and sins of every one of us!

Romans 3:23 (NLT) For everyone has sinned; we all fall short of God's glorious standard.

Romans 6:23 (NLT) For the wages of sin is death, but the free gift of God is eternal life through Christ Jesus our Lord.

Romans 5:8 (NLT) But God showed His great love for us by sending Christ to die for us while we were still sinners.

Acts 4:12 (TLB) There is salvation in no one else! Under all heaven there is no other name for men to call upon to save them.

John 3:16–17 (TLB) For God loved the world so much that he gave his only Son so that anyone who believes in him shall not perish but have eternal life. God did not send his Son into the world to condemn it, but to save it.

Ephesians 2:4–5 (TLB) But God is so rich in mercy; he loved us so much that even though we were spiritually dead and doomed by our sins, he gave us back our lives again when he raised Christ from the dead—only by his undeserved favor have we ever been saved.

1 John 1:9 (TLB) But if we confess our sins to him, he can be depended on to forgive us and to cleanse us from every wrong. And it is perfectly proper for God to do this for us because Christ died to wash away our sins.*

Ephesians 2:8–9 (TLB) Because of his kindness, you have been saved through trusting Christ. And even trusting is not of yourselves; it too is a gift from God. Salvation is not a reward for the good we have done, so none of us can take any credit for it.

Romans 10:9–10 (TLB) For if you tell others with your own mouth that Jesus Christ is your Lord and believe in your own heart that God has raised him from the dead, you will be saved. For it is by believing in his heart that a man becomes right with God; and with his mouth he tells others of his faith, confirming his salvation.

1 John 5:13–15 (TLB) I have written this to you who believe in the Son of God so that you may know you have eternal life. And we are sure of this, that he will listen to us whenever we ask him for anything in line with his will. And if we really know he is listening when we talk to him and make our requests, then we can be sure that he will answer us.

2 Timothy 3:16–17 (TLB) The whole Bible was given to us by inspiration from God and is useful to teach us what is true and to make us realize what is wrong in our lives; it straightens us out and helps us do what is right. It is God's way of making us well prepared at every point, fully equipped to do good to everyone.

Psalm 19:7–11 (TLB) God's laws are perfect. They protect us, make us wise, and give us joy and light. God's laws are pure, eternal, just. They are more desirable than gold. They are sweeter than honey dripping from a honeycomb. For they warn us away from harm and give success to those who obey them.

Galatians 5:16–23 (TLB) I advise you to obey only the Holy Spirit's instructions. He will tell you where to go and what to do, and then you won't always be doing the wrong things your evil nature wants you to. For we naturally love to do evil things that are just the opposite from the things that the Holy Spirit tells us to do; and the good things we want to do when the

Spirit has his way with us are just the opposite of our natural desires. These two forces within us are constantly fighting each other to win control over us, and our wishes are never free from their pressures. When you are guided by the Holy Spirit, you need no longer force yourself to obey Jewish laws.

But when you follow your own wrong inclinations, your lives will produce these evil results: impure thoughts, eagerness for lustful pleasure, idolatry, spiritism (that is, encouraging the activity of demons), hatred and fighting, jealousy and anger, constant effort to get the best for yourself, complaints and criticisms, the feeling that everyone else is wrong except those in your own little group—and there will be wrong doctrine, envy, murder, drunkenness, wild parties, and all that sort of thing. Let me tell you again, as I have before, that anyone living that sort of life will not inherit the Kingdom of God.

But when the Holy Spirit controls our lives he will produce this kind of fruit in us: love, joy, peace, patience, kindness, goodness, faithfulness, gentleness and self-control; and here there is no conflict with Jewish laws.

Colossians 3:12–17 (TLB) Since you have been chosen by God who has given you this new kind of life, and because of his deep love and concern for you, you should practice tenderhearted mercy and kindness to others. Don't worry about making a good impression on them, but be ready to suffer quietly and patiently. Be gentle and ready to forgive; never hold grudges. Remember, the Lord forgave you, so you must forgive others.

Most of all, let love guide your life, for then the whole church will stay together in perfect harmony. Let the peace of heart that comes from Christ be always present in your hearts and lives, for this is your responsibility and privilege as members of his body. And always be thankful.

Remember what Christ taught, and let his words enrich your lives and make you wise; teach them to each other and sing them out in psalms and hymns and spiritual songs, singing to the Lord with thankful hearts. And whatever you do or say, let it be as a representative of the Lord Jesus, and come with him into the presence of God the Father to give him your thanks.

Philippians 2:13 (TLB) For God is at work within you, helping you want to obey him, and then helping you do what he wants.

John 10:27–29 (TLB) My sheep recognize my voice, and I know them, and they follow me. I give them eternal life and they shall never perish. No one shall snatch them away from me, for my Father has given them to me, and he is more powerful than anyone else, so no one can kidnap them from me.

Isaiah 41:10 (TLB) Fear not, for I am with you. Do not be dismayed. I am your God. I will strengthen you; I will help you; I will uphold you with my victorious right hand.

Deuteronomy 31:6 (TLB) Be strong! Be courageous! Do not be afraid of them! For the Lord your God will be with you. He will neither fail you nor forsake you.

Bibliography

Batura, Paul. "Beware the Images Culture is Placing on the Minds of Our Children." *Daily Citizen*, March 8, 2022. https://dailycitizen.focusonthefamily.com/beware-the-images-culture-is-placing-on-the-minds-of-our-children/.

Dobson, James C., and Gary L. Bauer, *Children at Risk: The Battle for the Hearts and Minds of Our Kids*. Nashville: Thomas Nelson, Inc., 1990.

Ortland, Dane. *Gentle and Lowly: The Heart of Christ for Sinners and Sufferers*. Wheaton, IL: Crossway/Good News Publishers, 2021.

Roberts, Candyce. *Help for the Fractured Soul*. Ada, MI: Chosen Books, 2012.

CPSIA information can be obtained
at www.ICGtesting.com
Printed in the USA
LVHW041159261022
731593LV00003B/443

9 781955 043915